A Musical

Book and Lyrics by
BILL RUSSELL

Music by
HENRY KRIEGER

Original Broadway Production
Directed and Choreographed by
ROBERT LONGBOTTOM

SAMUEL FRENCH, INC.
45 West 25th Street   NEW YORK 10010
7623 Sunset Boulevard HOLLYWOOD 90046
LONDON   TORONTO

SIDE SHOW, book and lyrics by Bill Russell and music by Henry Krieger, orchestrations by Harold Wheeler, vocal and dance arrangements and music direction by David Chase, scenic design by Robin Wagner, costume design by Gregg Barnes, lighting design by Brian MacDevitt, sound design by Tom Clark, production stage manager Perry Cline, musical coordination Seymour Red Press, associate choreographer Tom Kosis, directed and choreographed by Robert Longbottom, presented by Emanuel Azenberg, Joseph Nederlander, Herschel Waxman, Janice McKenna and Scott Nederlander, premiered at the Richard Rodgers Theater on October 16, 1997 with the following cast and musicians:

CAST
(in alphabetical order)

Reptile Man	BARRY FINKEL
Bearded Lady	ANDY GALE
Roustabout	BILLY HARTUNG
Snake Lady	EMILY HSU
Fortune Teller	ALICIA IRVING
Fakir	DEVANAND N. JANKI
The Boss	KEN JENNINGS
Jake	NORM LEWIS
6th Exhibit	JUDY MALLOY
Sheik	DAVID MASENHEIMER
Terry Connor	JEFF McCARTHY
Roustabout	DAVID McDONALD
Geek	PHILLIP OFFICER
Buddy Foster	HUGH PANARO
Dolly Dimples	VERNA PIERCE
Violet Hilton	ALICE RIPLEY
Roustabout	JIM T. RUTTMAN
Daisy Hilton	EMILY SKINNER
Harem Girl	JENNY-LYNN SUCKLING
Harem Girl	SUSAN TAYLOR
Roustabout	TIMOTHY WARMEN
Harem Girl	DARLENE WILSON

The **SIDE SHOW** cast also plays Reporters, Vaudevillians, the Follies Company, Party Guests, Radio Show Singers and Hawkers.

PRODUCTION NOTE

In the Broadway production of SIDE SHOW, Daisy and Violet's connection was created by the two actors standing side by side. They were never literally connected by corsets, velcro or any other costume piece. This allowed the audience to participate in creating the twins' connection with their collective imagination and made the actor's achievement of appearing to be joined all the more impressive (especially when dancing).

The characters of the Roustabouts were partly conceived to assist in helping with onstage set changes. Specific points where they do so are indicated in the script.

MUSICAL NUMBERS

ACT I

The Midway

Come Look At The Freaks ....The Boss and Company
Like Everyone Else ....Daisy and Violet
You Deserve A Better Life ....Buddy and Terry
Crazy, Deaf and Blind ....The Boss
The Devil You Know ....Jake and Attractions
More Than We Bargained For ....Buddy and Terry
Feelings You've Got To Hide ....Daisy and Violet
When I'm By Your Side ....Daisy and Violet
Say Goodbye To The Freak Show ....The Company

Vaudeville

Overnight Sensation ....Terry and Reporters
Leave Me Alone ....Daisy and Violet
We Share Everything ....Daisy, Violet and Vaudevillians
The Interview ....Daisy, Violet and Reporters
Who Will Love Me As I Am ....Daisy and Violet

ACT II

The Follies

Rare Songbirds On Display ....The Company
New Year's Day .....Terry, Buddy, Jake, Daisy, Violet and Company
Private Conversation ....Terry

On The Road

One Plus One Equals Three ....Buddy, Daisy, Violet
You Should Be Loved ....Jake

The Texas Centennial

Tunnel Of Love ....Terry, Buddy, Daisy, Violet
Beautiful Day For A Wedding ....The Boss and Hawkers
Marry Me, Terry ....Daisy
I Will Never Leave You ....Daisy and Violet
Finale ....The Company

ACT I

Scene 1
PROLOGUE

(The COMPANY, costumed as average citizens of the 1930s, enters and sits facing the audience. There is a moment of silence as the COMPANY and audience stare at each other. Then softly the music begins and the COMPANY starts to sing.)

(#1 "Come Look at the Freaks")

COMPANY.
COME LOOK AT THE FREAKS
COME GAPE AT THE GEEKS
COME EXAMINE THESE ABERRATIONS
THEIR MALFORMATIONS
GROTESQUE PHYSIQUES
ONLY PENNIES FOR PEEKS
COME LOOK AT THE FREAKS

MEN.	**WOMEN.**
COME LOOK AT THE FREAKS	AH, AH, AH
THEY'LL HAUNT YOU FOR WEEKS	(Etc.)
COME EXPLORE WHY THEY	
FASCINATE YOU	
EXASPERATE YOU	
AND FLUSH YOUR CHEEKS	

WOMEN.
COME HEAR HOW LOVE SPEAKS
ALL.
COME LOOK AT THE FREAKS

(An ACTOR stands and becomes THE BOSS. As he introduces his attractions, ACTORS stand and become the acts he's describing.)

7

THE BOSS.
LADIES AND GENTLEMEN
STEP RIGHT UP
RIGHT THIS WAY
THERE IS NO WAIT
WE DON'T WASTE YOUR TIME
SO LITTLE TO PAY
JUST ONE THIN DIME
GAINS YOU ADMISSION
TO MY ODDITORIUM
NEVER HAVE YOU SEEN
A COMPARABLE EMPORIUM
OF WONDERS UNDER ONE TENT
YOUR DIME COULD NOT BE BETTER SPENT

COME SEE A CURIOUS GAL
THE BEARDED LADY
SEE A MAN TURNED INTO A REPTILE
AS PUNISHMENT FOR HIS SINS
COME HEAR THE HAUNTING SONG
OF THE SIAMESE TWINS

COME SEE OUR ELEGANT GEEK
REFINED BUT DEADLY
CHICKEN NECKS DELIGHT HIS INCISORS
THEIR HEADS DECORATE THE MUD
HIS FAV'RITE COCKTAIL DRINK?
IT'S WARM CHICKEN BLOOD!

FROM THE BARREN DESERT
OF THE HEATHEN CAMEL TRADE
FOR OUR GENTLEMEN FRIENDS
THE SERAGLIO OF A HASHEMITE SHEIK
HIS HAREM WAS FREED
AND WE HAVE FOUND IT'S QUITE UNIQUE
FOR THESE GIRLS ARE VIRGINS STILL
HAD I ARRIVED BUT AN HOUR LATE
THAT OLD SHEIK WOULD HAVE HAD HIS FILL
    ALL.
COME SEE GOD'S MISTAKES
THE FREAKS GOD FORSAKES
TAKE A LOOK AT THE MONSTER BABIES
DOG MEN WITH RABIES

ALL. (Cont.)
A BRIDE OF SNAKES
   THE BOSS.
AND WE DON'T HARBOR FAKES
   ALL.
COME SEE GOD'S MISTAKES

(JAKE, an African-American man, stands)

   THE BOSS.
FROM THE INKY JUNGLES
OF THE DARKEST CONTINENT
YOU WILL WITNESS FIRSTHAND
THE FEROCITY OF THE CANNIBAL KING
WE KEEP HIM CHAINED UP
BECAUSE WE KNOW HE'S HANKERING
FOR A TASTE OF ONE OF YOU
AND YOU ARE HERE FOR ENLIGHTENMENT
NOT AS STOCK FOR CANNIBAL STEW

   THE BOSS.
COME LOOK AT THE FREAKS

COME GAPE AT THE GEEKS

COME EXAMINE THESE
   ABERRATIONS
THEIR MALFORMATIONS
GROTESQUE PHYSIQUES

ONLY PENNIES FOR PEEKS

   ATTRACTIONS.

COME INSIDE

CURIOSITY SATISFIED
COME! ...

SEE THE UNDERSIDE

AH, AH, INSIDE ...
AH ...

The COMPANY goes "inside" the tent leaving DAISY and VIOLET.)

   THE BOSS.
WON'T YOU PLEASE FORGIVE ME
IF I SEEM EMOTIONAL
FOR THE STARS OF OUR SHOW
I AM SPEAKING OF COURSE
OF THE SIAMESE TWINS

THE BOSS. (Cont.)
I ADOPTED THESE GIRLS
AND GAVE THEM MORAL DISCIPLINES
TAUGHT THEM STANDARDS
RIGHT FROM WRONG
I NURTURED THEIR MUSICALITY
LET THEM CHARM YOU WITH THEIR SONG

(DAISY and VIOLET cross Downstage, face each other and sing.)

DAISY and VIOLET.
AH, AH, AH (Etc.)

(DAISY and VIOLET face front, connect, pivot Upstage and enter the tent, now conjoined at the hip. Four ROUSTABOUTS help create the Midway side of the tent.)

Scene 1A - THE MIDWAY

THE BOSS. Ladies and gentlemen, step right up. Right this way. See the freaks. They're here. They're real. They're all alive. Inside!

(As THE BOSS continues, BUDDY enters, followed shortly by TERRY.)

BUDDY.
THIS WAY, MR. CONNOR, OVER HERE.
TERRY.
WHERE ARE WE GOING?
BUDDY.
TO A SHOWING OF THE SIAMESE TWINS.
TERRY. Siamese twins?
BUDDY.
I WANT YOU TO HEAR THEM SING.
TERRY. Siamese twins?
BUDDY.
WE'RE JUST IN TIME.
LET'S GO INSIDE

TERRY.
IS THIS SOME KIND OF JOKE?
BUDDY.
NOT AT ALL.
TERRY. Good.
BECAUSE I'M A VERY BUSY MAN ...
BUDDY.
YOU WON'T BE DISAPPOINTED
THIS COULD PAY OFF BIG
FOR BOTH OF US
TERRY.
HOW?
BUDDY.
FIRST YOU HAVE TO SEE THEM
TERRY.
I DON'T LIKE THIS PLACE.
BUDDY.
BUT WE'RE HERE
WE MIGHT AS WELL STAY
I'LL EVEN PAY
TERRY.
OKAY
I'LL HELP YOU SPEND
YOUR HARD-EARNED DOUGH
BUT THIS IS NOT MY KIND OF SHOW
THE BOSS.
LET ME ALLAY YOUR FRIGHT
THE ATTRACTIONS DON'T BITE
COME INSIDE

*(The ROUSTABOUTS help create the inside of the tent. BUDDY
    and TERRY take seats Stage Left as the HAREM GIRLS and
    SHEIK enter and perform an erotic dance.)*

*(# 1A **"Come Look at the Freaks"**)*

Scene 1B - INSIDE THE TENT

(The ATTRACTIONS present brief portions of their acts: the GEEK mimes biting off a chicken's head, the REPTILE MAN slithers and crawls, the FAKIR charms the SNAKE LADY, the FORTUNE TELLER conjures, the BEARDED LADY preens, DOLLY DIMPLES laughs maniacally while displaying her amplitude, and, finally, the CANNIBAL KING is "tamed" by the ROUSTABOUTS and THE BOSS. He breaks free and terrorizes TERRY. The ROUSTABOUTS "recapture" him and drag him off.)

THE BOSS. Ladies and gentlemen, no cause for alarm—the Cannibal King has been subdued and is under our control. There is nothing to fear. Please remain in your seats to experience our premiere attraction in its most revealing display. *(DAISY and VIOLET are revealed in silhouette.)* Scientists believe that Siamese twins come from the same life germ and that their complete separation was retarded in some way—perhaps, while pregnant, their mother witnessed dogs stuck together copulating. They are called "Siamese" because Chang and Eng, the first widely known specimens, came from Siam. Siamese twins share everything—yet remain completely separate in their minds, bodily functions and, presumably, their souls. But enough about science. Sing, girls, sing!

DAILY & VIOLET.
AHH AHHHH AHHHH (Etc.)

THE BOSS.	**ALL.**
COME LOOK AT THE FREAKS	
	COME INSIDE
COME GAPE AT THE GEEKS	
	CURIOSITY SATISFIED

THE BOSS & ALL.
COME EXAMINE THESE ABERRATIONS
THEIR MALFORMATIONS
GROTESQUE PHYSIQUES
ONLY PENNIES FOR PEEKS
COME LOOK AT THE FREAKS!

Scene 2 - ON THE MIDWAY

(The ROUSTABOUTS help adjust the set back to Midway position, as BUDDY and TERRY exit tent.)

(#2 "On the Midway")

BUDDY.
I'M DYING TO KNOW WHAT YOU THINK
TERRY.
I'M INTRIGUED ...
BUDDY. Great!
TERRY.
WHY DID YOU BRING ME HERE?
BUDDY.
THOSE TWINS—THEY HAVE SOMETHING
TERRY.
SOMETHING I'LL NEVER FORGET
BUDDY.
I COULD HELP THEM CREATE AN ACT
AND YOU COULD GET THEM TO VAUDEVILLE
TERRY.
WHAT KIND OF ACT?
BUDDY.
SINGING SIAMESE TWINS!
TERRY. You call that singing?
BUDDY. Not exactly. But I could teach them. Look what I did with the Nubian Nightingale.
TERRY. She needed help.
BUDDY.
I COULD REALLY HELP THOSE GIRLS
TEACH THEM TO SING
MAYBE TO DANCE
TERRY. Dance! You certainly don't lack confidence.
BUDDY. I like a challenge. You wouldn't believe some of the acts I've helped.
TERRY. Yeah. I know. You're very ambitious—for an usher.

BUDDY.
BUT I CAN DO A LOT MORE
AND YOU CAN GIVE ME MY BREAK
TERRY.
WITH THOSE TWINS?
BUDDY.
EXACTLY
TERRY.
WELL I HAVE TO ADMIT
THERE'S SOMETHING ABOUT THOSE GIRLS
BUDDY.
LET'S MEET THEM
TERRY. Okay.
BUDDY. Great! But there is one problem ...
TERRY.
ONE?
BUDDY. The owner keeps them under lock and key.
TERRY.
LEAVE HIM TO ME
BUDDY. Gladly.
TERRY.
AND IF WE GET TO MEET THEM
LET ME DO THE TALKING
BUDDY.
WHATEVER YOU SAY
THE BOSS. *(Entering.)*
THAT WAS OUR LAST SHOW TODAY
BUT WOULD YOU GENTLEMEN
LIKE TO SEE MORE?
TERRY.
MORE?
THE BOSS.
MORE OF THE SIAMESE TWINS
TERRY. Could we?
THE BOSS.
THEY MIGHT BE CONVINCED
TO DISPLAY THEIR CONNECTION
UP CLOSE AND PRIVATE
FOR A SMALL CONSIDERATION
TERRY.
CONSIDERATION?

THE BOSS.
TWO BUCKS FOR TEN MINUTES
TOTAL EXPOSURE OF THE FLESHY LINK
  But no touching!
YOU'RE IN
FOR THE EXPERIENCE OF A LIFETIME
RIGHT THIS WAY

(The ROUSTABOUTS help change the set to suggest the area behind the tent.)

Scene 3 - BEHIND THE TENT

(The ATTRACTIONS enter from Upstage, leading DAISY and VIO-LET to a bench.)

(#3 "Attention, Ladies and Gentlemen")

GEEK.
ATTENTION, LADIES AND GENTLEMEN
YOUR ATTENTION PLEASE
THE CANNIBAL KING
WHO BEING THE ONLY ROYALTY AROUND ...
  BEARDED LADY. Says who?
  GEEK.
HIS POSTER
HIS BILLING
SAY HE'S A KING
  BEARDED LADY. Mine says I'm a lady.
  REPTILE MAN. They had to call you something.
  GEEK. As I was saying ...
THE CANNIBAL KING
WISHES TO MAKE
A PROCLAMATION
ALL HEAR THE CANNIBAL KING!
  JAKE.
I
BEING THE ONLY AVAILABLE KING
HEREBY DECLARE TODAY A HOLIDAY

JAKE. (Cont.)
TO HONOR
THE MOST BEAUTIFUL MAIDENS
IN THE LAND
ON THE BIRTHDAY THEY SHARE
ALONG WITH EVERYTHING ELSE
INCLUDING OUR LOVE
  ALL.
HAPPY BIRTHDAY TO YOU AND TO YOU
HERE'S A BIG HAPPY BIRTHDAY TIMES TWO
HAPPY BIRTHDAY FROM THE WHOLE DAMNED CREW
HAPPY BIRTHDAY TO YOU AND TO YOU

(THE BOSS enters with TERRY and BUDDY following.)

  THE BOSS. Okay. Party's over. The Twins have a private appointment.
  GEEK. But it's their birthday.
  THE BOSS. Says who?
  FORTUNE TELLER. We've always had a little celebration on...
  THE BOSS. I'm trying to run a business here.

(#3A "We've Got a Customer")

WE'VE GOT A CUSTOMER
WHO WANTS A PRIVATE SHOW
AND THE CUSTOMER'S ALWAYS RIGHT
  The rest of you out of my sight.

(The ATTRACTIONS "disappear" from the immediate area but remain where they can see what's happening. BUDDY also keeps his distance.)

  JAKE.
BOSS
THE DAY'S RECEIPTS
ARE IN THE TIN
AND I GOTCHA
A BRAND NEW BOTTLE OF GIN
  THE BOSS. Good. You stay here, Jake. Mister, you got ten minutes.

(THE BOSS exits.)

DAISY. *(To VIOLET, starting to unbutton her dress.)* Happy birthday.

VIOLET. *(To DAISY, also unbuttoning.)* Happy birthday.

TERRY. Wait. You don't have to show me anything. I just want to talk.

JAKE. You made a deal to look, not to talk.

TERRY. Here. I'll give you all the cash I've got on me.

(#3B "Behind the Bleachers")

JAKE.
MISTER
I LIKE MONEY AS MUCH AS ANYBODY
BUT IN THIS DEPRESSION
I LIKE MY JOB EVEN MORE

TERRY.
THEY HAVE NOTHING TO FEAR FROM ME

JAKE.
GOOD
'CAUSE EVEN MORE THAN MY JOB
I LIKE THESE GIRLS

TERRY. Then you'll like what I can do for them. I only want a couple minutes of private conversation.

JAKE.
IF THE BOSS COMES BACK ...

TERRY. Over there you can keep an eye out for him and an eye on me at the same time.

DAISY.
HE SEEMS OKAY, JAKE

VIOLET.
YOU'LL BE NEARBY

JAKE.
I DON'T LIKE IT

VIOLET.
FOR ME, JAKE

JAKE.
I CAN'T SAY NO TO YOU

(JAKE moves away but remains visible.)

DAISY.
WHO ARE YOU?

TERRY.
NAME'S TERRY CONNOR
I HAVE BUSINESS TO DISCUSS
    VIOLET.
ARE YOU SURE YOU MEAN WITH US?
    TERRY.
YES
AND LET ME ASSURE YOU
I HAVE HONORABLE AIMS
BUT FIRST WHAT ARE YOUR NAMES?
    DAISY.
I'M DAISY
    VIOLET.
I'M VIOLET
    DAISY and VIOLET.
WE'RE SIAMESE TWINS
    TERRY.
SO I NOTICED
WHAT'S THAT LIKE?
    DAISY.
WHAT'S IT LIKE BEING HANDSOME?
    VIOLET. You're being rude.
    DAISY. Am not.
    TERRY.
I WAS RUDE TO ASK.
    VIOLET. Everyone does.
    TERRY. But you must be very similar. Right ... I'm sorry, which one is ... ?
    DAISY.
I'M DAISY
    VIOLET.
I'M VIOLET
    DAISY and VIOLET.
WE'RE NOTHING ALIKE
    VIOLET.
I'M TO YOUR RIGHT
AS YOU WATCH OUR SHOW
    DAISY.
SHE THINKS SHE'S ALWAYS RIGHT
NOT SO
I'M DAISY

VIOLET.
I'M VIOLET
DAISY and VIOLET.
WHAT ELSE WOULD YOU LIKE TO KNOW?
TERRY. Which one makes the most decisions?
DAISY.
I DO
VIOLET.
I DO
DAISY and VIOLET.
WE BOTH MAKE OUR OWN DECISIONS
TERRY.
THERE MUST BE TIMES YOU DON'T AGREE
DAISY.
NOT ME
VIOLET.
NOT ME
TERRY.
OR TIMES YOU WANT TO BE ALONE
VIOLET.
THEN WE CLOSE A DOOR INSIDE
AND HIDE
TERRY.
BUT WHERE?
VIOLET.
IN A SECRET PLACE WE KNOW
WHERE NOBODY ELSE CAN GO
TERRY.
HOW?
DAISY.
HAVEN'T YOU EVER
BEEN IN CONVERSATION
AND YOUR MIND DRIFTED SOMEWHERE ELSE?
VIOLET.
OR BEEN IN A ROOM
SURROUNDED BY PEOPLE
AND YET FELT A MILLION MILES AWAY?
TERRY.
I GUESS I HAVE
DAISY.
WELL THAT'S WHERE WE GO
WHEN WE WANT TO BE ALONE

VIOLET.
WE COULD GO THERE RIGHT NOW
IF YOU WANTED US TO
    DAISY.
BUT WE'D RATHER STAY WITH YOU
    TERRY. Good!
I WAS TAKEN WITH YOUR SINGING
YOU HAVE TALENT
POTENTIAL
TO DO MUCH MORE
    DAISY.
BUT WE'RE FREAKS

(#4 "Like Everyone Else")

    TERRY.
YOU ARE UNUSUAL
EXOTIC
DIFF'RENT
UNIQUE
BUT MY TIME'S ALMOST UP
SO WILL YOU ALLOW
ONE QUESTION MORE
WHAT ARE YOUR DREAMS
WHAT ARE YOU LONGING FOR?
    VIOLET.
I WANT TO BE LIKE EVERYONE ELSE
SO NO ONE WILL POINT AND STARE
TO WALK DOWN THE STREET
NOT ATTRACTING ATTENTION
NO NOTICE, NO MENTION
NO HINT OF DESPAIR
A NORMAL REACTION
A STANDARD RESPONSE
THE SAME AS EVERYONE WANTS
    DAISY.
I WANT TO BE LIKE EVERYONE ELSE
BUT RICHER AND MORE ACCLAIMED
WORSHIPED AND CELEBRATED
PAMPERED AND LOVED
TO SEE THOSE WHO'VE LAUGHED
FEELING ASHAMED

DAISY. (Cont.)
A GLORIOUS, FRANTIC
ADORING RESPONSE
THE SAME AS EVERYONE WANTS

I'D GO ABROAD
SEE ALL THE SIGHTS
HEAR FOLKS APPLAUD
BOW TO THE LIGHTS
   VIOLET.
I'D SETTLE DOWN
NEVER TO ROAM
FIND A NICE HUSBAND AND HOME
   DAISY.
I WANT TO BE
   VIOLET.
I WANT TO BE
   DAISY and VIOLET.
LIKE EVERYONE ELSE
BUT NOT LIKE MY SISTER SAYS
   DAISY.
SHE WANTS STABILITY
   VIOLET.
SHE WOULD LIKE FAME
I'D LIKE SERENITY
   DAISY.
FRENZIED ACCLAIM
   DAISY and VIOLET.
THOUGH WE CAN'T AGREE ON A SINGLE RESPONSE
WE WANT WHAT EVERYONE WANTS
ONLY WHAT EVERYONE WANTS
THE SAME AS EVERYONE WANTS
   JAKE. Okay, time's up.
MISTER
YOU'D BETTER GET OUT OF HERE
   DAISY.
NO!
DON'T MAKE HIM GO
   JAKE.
IF THE BOSS COMES BACK ...
   TERRY.
GO GET HIM
I'D LIKE TO TALK TO HIM

JAKE. You don't know what you're getting into.
TERRY.
I ALWAYS KNOW
VIOLET.
PLEASE, JAKE
JAKE.
YOU TWO ARE GONNA LOSE ME MY JOB

(JAKE exits.)

DAISY. This is fun. Any more questions?
TERRY. Not for now.
VIOLET. Could we ask you one?
TERRY. Of course.
DAISY and VIOLET. Why are you here?
TERRY. Well, I admit I never expected to be, but a certain young man insisted I see you. Buddy, come here. This is Buddy Foster—a very talented musician.
BUDDY. I sing too.
TERRY. Yes he does.
BUDDY. And dance!
TERRY. All of that. Skip your resume. You tell them why we're here.

(#5 "You Deserve a Better Life")

BUDDY.
WHEN I HAPPENED UPON THIS SIDESHOW
I SAID "THEY NEED A MORE DIGNIFIED SHOW"
I FELT THE WAY YOU WERE PRESENTED
WAS COMPLETELY WRONG
AND WHEN I HEARD YOUR VOICES
I SAID "THEY NEED A SONG"

YOU DESERVE A BETTER LIFE
NO MORE WORRY, NO MORE STRIFE
FOR YOU POSSESS A GIFT TO CHERISH
IN THIS JUNGLE YOU COULD PERISH
WE'LL CUT THROUGH IT LIKE A KNIFE
YOU DESERVE A BETTER LIFE

(THE BOSS enters with JAKE.)

THE BOSS. You should be long gone. That was our deal.

TERRY. I'd like to make you a new and better one.

I'M IMPRESSED BY YOUR OPERATION
AND LET ME SAY
MY APPRECIATION OF YOUR HARD WORK
AND BUSINESS KNOW-HOW
COMES FROM YEARS MYSELF
IN LOW-BROW SITUATIONS
TRYING TO MAKE A BUCK

THE BOSS. Low-brow?

TERRY.

YOU DESERVE A BETTER LIFE
NO MORE WORRY, NO MORE STRIFE
FOR YOU POSSESS A GIFT TO CHERISH
IN THIS JUNGLE THEY COULD PERISH
I'LL CUT THROUGH IT LIKE A KNIFE
YOU DESERVE A BETTER LIFE

I could make you a lot of money.

THE BOSS. How?

TERRY. I'm a talent scout and press agent for the Orpheum circuit.

(# 5A "Your Girls Could Play Vaudeville")

TERRY.
YOUR GIRLS COULD PLAY VAUDEVILLE

DAISY.
VAUDEVILLE!

THE BOSS.
THEY'RE FREAKS

TERRY.
BUT THEY SING

THE BOSS. Caterwauling.

TERRY.
LET ME WORK WITH THEM

DAISY.
OH PLEASE LET US!

VIOLET.
MAYBE WE COULD LEARN SOMETHING

TERRY.
THIS FELLAH HERE
IS VERY GOOD
AT TEACHING HOW TO ...

THE BOSS. Stop! Could I ask you a question?
TERRY. Of course.
THE BOSS.
ARE YOU DEAF?
TERRY. No.
THE BOSS.
IF YOU THINK THESE GIRLS ARE SINGERS
THEN YOU MUST HAVE LOST YOUR HEARING
THEY DO A LITTLE YOWLING
DOGS BAYING AT THE MOON

BUT THE SOUND THEY MAKE IS SCREECHING
AND YOU'RE REALLY OVERREACHING
IF YOU THINK THESE LOUSY HONKERS
COULD EVER LEARN A TUNE
Oh. One other question.
TERRY. Yes?
THE BOSS.
ARE YOU BLIND?
IS THAT WHY YOU DIDN'T NOTICE
THAT THESE TWO ARE JOINED TOGETHER
WITH A LITTLE FLESH BETWEEN THEM
MAKING IT IMPOSSIBLE
TO GO IN TWO DIRECTIONS
OR INTO DIFFERENT SECTIONS
OF THE ROOM

I DON'T KNOW WHAT WEIRD PERVERSION
MAKES YOU FIND THESE DREGS EXCITING
BUT I PROTECT THEM
FROM VERMIN LIKE YOU
SO LET ME SAVE YOUR BREATH
AND MY VALUABLE TIME

THEY ARE FREAKS
THEY ARE MONSTERS
THEY WILL NEVER LEAVE THE SIDESHOW

AND THERE ARE OTHER PLAYTHINGS
WHICH I'M SURE THAT YOU CAN FIND
SO WHY DON'T YOU START LOOKING
THROUGH THE SLIME AND MUCK

THE BOSS. (Cont.)
GET IN IT
I CAN'T SPEND ANOTHER MINUTE
WITH SOMEONE CRAZY
DEAF
AND BLIND!
    TERRY. I apologize. Sorry to intrude.
    DAISY. Don't go.
    THE BOSS. Shut your mouth, you.
    TERRY. I don't mean to cause you trouble.
    THE BOSS. Well you have. Jake will show you off the grounds.

(#5B "So Lovely to meet you Ladies")

    TERRY.
SO LOVELY TO MEET YOU LADIES
    DAISY.
LOVELY
    VIOLET.
GOODBYE
    THE BOSS. Jake, make sure he gets gone. You girls get out of my
sight.

(THE BOSS exits.)

    TERRY. I'm right aren't I, Jake? They can sing.
    JAKE.
YES, THEY CAN
    TERRY.
THEN HELP ME PROVE THAT
    VIOLET.
HELP US, JAKE
    DAISY.
GIVE US A CHANCE TO LEARN
    JAKE.
YOU GIRLS WILL BE THE DEATH OF ME
YOU HEARD THE BOSS
    DAISY.
OH WHAT DOES HE KNOW
    DAISY.
HE'S A MEAN OLD DRUNK
    TERRY.
WE CAN CHANGE HIS TUNE

DAISY.
PLEASE, JAKE
VIOLET.
WE'LL BE VERY CAREFUL
DAISY.
HE DOESN'T NEED TO KNOW
VIOLET.
FOR ME, JAKE?
JAKE.
I CAN'T SAY NO TO YOU
TERRY. Good man. So—Buddy's going to teach you girls a song.
DAISY. I'm a quick learner.
TERRY. Great!
MY KIND OF GIRL
VIOLET.
I'M AFRAID YOU'LL HAVE
YOUR WORK CUT OUT WITH ME
BUDDY.
ALL YOU NEED IS A LITTLE HELP
VIOLET.
BUT WHAT IF I CAN'T DO THIS?
BUDDY.
I KNOW YOU CAN
TERRY. No pressure. You'll sing a song for us and maybe some
of your friends.
BUDDY.
SO DON'T WORRY
TERRY. Buddy will meet you here tomorrow night.
VIOLET.
WHAT ABOUT THE BOSS?
JAKE.
I'LL TAKE CARE OF HIM
DAISY.
WE'RE VERY GRATEFUL, JAKE
Will you be here tomorrow night, Mr. Connor?
TERRY.
CALL ME TERRY
I'LL BE BACK IN A COUPLE OF WEEKS
BUT I'LL BE THINKING OF YOU
WHILE I'M GONE

NOW WILL YOU GIRLS WORK VERY HARD
AND DO AS WE TELL YOU?

VIOLET.
OH YES WE WILL
DAISY.
ANYTHING YOU SAY
TERRY.
SAY GOOD-BYE TO THE FREAK SHOW
LET ME SHOW YOU A PLACE I KNOW
BUDDY.
WHERE ONLY DAISIES AND VIOLETS GROW
TERRY and BUDDY.
SAY GOOD-BYE TO THE FREAK SHOW
GOOD-BYE

(TERRY, BUDDY and JAKE exit.)

DAISY.
WHAT BROUGHT HIM HERE
THAT HANDSOME GUY?
VIOLET.
I WONDER WHAT
I WONDER WHY
DAISY.
DO YOU THINK HE COULD MAKE
OUR DREAMS COME TRUE?
VIOLET.
HE SURE WOULD HAVE A LOT OF WORK TO DO

(The ATTRACTIONS start emerging from "hiding".)

FORTUNE TELLER.
HE'S THE ONE TO DO IT
I CAN SEE IT ALL
SEE IT IN MY CRYSTAL BALL
DAISY. You heard what he said?
FORTUNE TELLER. Every word.
ROUSTABOUT 1. We all did.
BEARDED LADY.
DAISY AND VIOLET
PLEASE DON'T GO WITH THEM
6TH EXHIBIT.
NO
GIVE THEM A TRY!

DAISY.
WE'VE ALREADY AGREED TO
VIOLET.
AGREED TO LEARN A SONG
NOT TO LEAVE YOU
REPTILE MAN.
NOT YET
BEARDED LADY.
WE HEARD WHAT THEY SAID
SAY GOOD-BYE TO THE FREAK SHOW
VIOLET.
I WOULD NEVER DO THAT
DAISY.
I WOULD
NOT BECAUSE I WANT TO LEAVE YOU
BUT TO PLAY VAUDEVILLE
TO MAKE SOMETHING OF OUR LIVES
SHEIK.
THIS LIFE ISN'T GOOD ENOUGH FOR YOU?
HAREM GIRL 2.
YOU CALL THIS A LIFE?
GEEK.
I CALL THIS THE ONLY HOME
THE GIRLS HAVE EVER KNOWN
FAKIR.
PREDATORS WILL TARGET THEM
OUT THERE ON THEIR OWN
HAREM GIRL 3.
WELL I THINK THEY SHOULD GO
JAKE. *(Entering.)*
THAT'S ENOUGH
THIS IS NOT ABOUT ANY OF US
THIS IS THEIR DECISION

(#6 "The Devil You Know")

I'M NOT GONNA TELL YOU
YOU'RE MAKING A MISTAKE
TELL YOU NOT TO GO
NO I WON'T
I'LL ONLY SAY
WHAT I'VE LEARNED ALONG MY WAY

JAKE. (Cont.)
THE DEVIL YOU KNOW
BEATS THE DEVIL YOU DON'T

WE DON'T WORK
IN THE BEST OF SITUATIONS
WE DON'T LIVE VERY WELL
WE DON'T LIVE
IN THE NEIGHBORHOOD OF HEAVEN
WE LIVE SOMEWHERE CLOSER TO HELL

WE HAVE LEARNED
TO WORK AROUND THIS SITUATION
LEARNED TO HIDE
TILL THE HEAT HAS PASSED
YOU WILL LEARN
A PROMISE OF SALVATION
CAN MASK ANOTHER INFERNO'S BLAST

THE DEVIL YOU KNOW
BEATS THE DEVIL YOU DON'T
THAT PROMISED LAND
COULD TURN OUT TO BE DRY
ONCE YOU'RE GONE
YOU MIGHT ASK YOURSELVES WHY
MAYBE YOU WILL
OR MAYBE YOU WON'T
BUT THE DEVIL YOU KNOW
BEATS THE DEVIL YOU DON'T
OH YEAH!
    ROUSTABOUT 1.
YOU DON'T KNOW
THE WORLD BEYOND THE SIDESHOW
    ROUSTABOUT 2.
YOU DON'T KNOW
WHAT SATAN CAN PLAN
    BEARDED LADY.
YOU DON'T KNOW
THE SAFETY YOU'D BE LEAVING
    SHEIK.
WE'RE YOUR FAMILY
AND WE'RE YOUR CLAN

SNAKE LADY.
HERE WE'VE GOT
EACH OTHER TO DEPEND ON
   HAREM GIRL 2.
HERE YOU'VE GOT
THE BEST HOME YOU'LL EVER FIND
   BEARDED LADY.
OTHER FOLK
DON'T KNOW HOW TO TAKE US
   JAKE.
THE WORLD OUT THERE
CAN BE SO UNKIND
THE DEVIL YOU KNOW ...

        ROUSTABOUT 1.
        DEVIL YOU KNOW
        ROUSTABOUT 2.
        DEVIL YOU KNOW

BEATS THE DEVIL YOU DON'T   **SNAKE LADY,**
        BEARDED LADY,
        HAREM GIRL 2,
        ROUSTABOUT 2.
        BEATS THE DEVIL
        THE DEVIL
        YOU DON'T

HIS GAME OF CHANCE

        SHEIK.
   JAKE.   DON'T TAKE THAT CHANCE
JUST MIGHT BE A SCAM

        SHEIK, HAREM GIRL 2,
        SNAKE LADY
        IT'S JUST A SCAM

   JAKE, ROUSTABOUT 3.
YOU CAN'T PLAY
THEN DECIDE YOU SHOULD SCRAM
   JAKE, ROUSTABOUTS 1&3, SHEIK.
MAYBE YOU'LL WIN
OR MAYBE YOU WON'T
BUT THE DEVIL YOU KNOW

                                    BEARDED LADY,
                                    HAREM GIRL 2,
                                    ROUSTABOUT 2.
                        DEVIL YOU KNOW
ALL EIGHT (JAKE, ROUSTABOUTS 1,2,&3, HAREM GIRL 2
SNAKE LADY, BEARDED LADY, SHEIK).
BEATS THE DEVIL YOU DON'T
        6TH EXHIBIT.
HOW CAN YOU
SAY THAT MAN'S A DEVIL?
        ROUSTABOUT 4.
HOW CAN YOU
SAY HE'S WICKED AND BAD?
        GEEK.
HOW CAN YOU
CRITICIZE AN ANGEL?
        ALL THREE.
PROMISING MORE HEAVEN
THAN THEY'VE EVER HAD
        FORTUNE TELLER.
I'M A FORTUNE TELLER
I CAN SEE THE FUTURE
I CAN LOOK AT PEOPLE
SEE WHAT'S LYING AHEAD

VIOLET AND DAISY
I SEE YOU'RE BOUND FOR GLORY
THE MAN THAT WAS HERE
WILL DO ALL THAT HE SAID

THAT MAN'S NOT A DEVIL
NO—BELIEVE IT I WON'T
HE'S NOT A DEVIL NO ...
AN' MISS THIS CHANCE
I HOPE THAT THEY DON'T
NO DON'T
NO DON'T
NO DON'T
        THE NO GROUP (JAKE, ROUSTABOUTS 1,2&3, HAREM
        GIRL 2, SNAKE LADY, BEARDED LADY, SHEIK).
WHAT IF HE'S A DEVIL?

THE YES GROUP
(6TH EXHIBIT, GEEK, FORTUNE TELLER, DOLLY DIMPLES, REPTILE MAN, FAKIR, ROUST-ABOUT 4, HAREM GIRLS 1&2).
WHAT IF HE'S NOT?
HE COULD BE AN ANGEL

THE NO GROUP.
THAT HEAVEN FORGOT!
FORTUNE TELLER.
I THINK YOU MAY BE JEALOUS
JAKE.
JEALOUS OF WHAT?
ALL.
THAT VIOLET AND DAISY
MIGHT GIVE HIM A SHOT!
THE NO GROUP.
BUT THE DEVIL YOU KNOW

BEATS THE DEVIL YOU DON'T

THAT PROMISED LAND

COULD TURN OUT TO BE DRY

SO DRY—
ONCE YOU'RE GONE
YOU MIGHT ASK YOUR-
  SELVES WHY

MAYBE YOU WILL

BUT THE DEVIL YOU KNOW

BUT THE DEVIL YOU KNOW

BUT THE DEVIL YOU KNOW

THE YES GROUP.
HE'S NOT A DEVIL

I WON'T BELIEVE IT
BELIEVE IT I WON'T

UNDERSTAND

HE COULD BE A GOOD GUY

WHY?

OR MAYBE YOU WON'T

NO, NO, HE'S NOT A DEVIL

NO, NO, HE'S NOT A DEVIL

NO, NO, HE'S NOT A DEVIL

JAKE.
ALRIGHT
WE COULD ARGUE ALL NIGHT
BECAUSE WE CARE ABOUT YOU TWO
MAYBE YOU WILL GO
OR MAYBE YOU WON'T
BUT I HOPE YOU WILL REMEMBER
THAT THAT MEAN OLD
MONEY-GRUBBIN'
GIN-GUZZLIN'
NAME-CALLIN'
DEVIL YOU KNOW
MIGHT BE BETTER THAN
THAT SMOOTH-TALKIN'
FINE-LOOKIN'
DREAM-SPINNIN'
PROMISE-MAKIN'
DEVIL
YOU DON'T!
    THE YES GROUP.

NO, NO, NO	**THE NO GROUP.**
DON'T CALL HIM A DEVIL!	BEATS THE DEVIL YOU DON'T
NO, NO, NO	
DON'T CALL HIM A DEVIL!	BEATS THE DEVIL YOU DON'T
NO, NO, NO,	
DON'T CALL HIM A DEVIL!	BEATS THE DEVIL YOU

    ALL.
DON'T!

*(On applause, the ATTRACTIONS exit Upstage as the ROUST-
ABOUTS help change the set to the inside of the tent.)*

Scene 4 - IN THE TENT

(#7 "More Than We Bargained For")

    TERRY. *(Entering.)*
SOME HIDDEN MAGNET
IS PULLING ME BACK

TERRY. (Cont.)
BACK TO THIS STRANGE LITTLE SHOW
AN INVISIBLE FORCE
DRAGGING ME OFF-COURSE
PULLING ME SOMEWHERE
I KNOW I SHOULDN'T GO

I WANT, I WANT
I WANT TO SEE HER
I WANT, I WANT TO LOOK AT HER FACE
I NEED, I NEED
I NEED TO SEE HER
THAT'S WHY I'M BACK IN THIS PLACE

(BUDDY enters with JAKE.)

    BUDDY. Mr. Connor! Thank God you're back.
    TERRY. Hey, Buddy. Everything okay?
    BUDDY.
BETTER THAN THAT
JAKE, TELL THE GIRLS
MR. CONNOR IS HERE

(JAKE exits.)

    TERRY.
LET'S GO SEE THEM
    BUDDY.
THEY'RE NOT QUITE DRESSED
WE HAD TO WAIT
TILL THE BOSS PASSED OUT
    TERRY.
ARE THEY READY TO PERFORM?
    BUDDY.
WE CAN'T WAIT TO SHOW YOU
THE WORK WE'VE ACCOMPLISHED
YOU WON'T BELIEVE YOUR OWN EYES
MEETING EACH NIGHT
AT THE ODDEST OF HOURS
BUT OH HOW EACH HOUR FLIES
OUR TWO GIRLS HAVE SPECIAL GIFT
I'VE ONLY BEGUN TO EXPLORE
ANY CLOUDS OF DOUBT WILL LIFT

BUDDY. (Cont.)
I THINK WE'RE GETTING MORE
THAN WE BARGAINED FOR
    TERRY. We'll see about that. Sounds like you've managed okay here.
    BUDDY.
WORKING IN THE MIDST OF THE STRANGEST FOLKS
THEY'RE HELPFUL
I LIKE THEM
THEY GET MY JOKES
I THOUGHT THEY WERE PERFORMERS
IN A SAD, BLEAK SHOW
BUT HERE I AM
I FIT RIGHT IN
INTO A FREAK SHOW!
    TERRY. So, Buddy, you finally found a home. Have the girls
given you any trouble?
    BUDDY.
WELL VIOLET IS SLOW
BUT WE WORK TILL SHE GETS IT
DAISY DOES EVERYTHING RIGHT
I'M MORE CONCERNED
WITH SOME PERSONAL QUESTIONS
I SWEAR I DID NOT INVITE
I THINK VIOLET'S SWEET ON ME
SWEET'S VERY HARD TO IGNORE
DAISY MENTIONS YOU WITH GLEE
I THINK WE'RE GETTING MORE
THAN WE BARGAINED FOR
    TERRY. Daisy asks about me?
    BUDDY. Only about fifty times a day.
    TERRY. You're kidding.
SHE THINKS I'LL MAKE HER FAMOUS
GET HER FOOT IN THE DOOR
    BUDDY.
I THINK WE'RE GETTING MORE
THAN WE BARGAINED FOR
DO YOU THINK THEY'RE PRETTY?
    TERRY.
PRETTY?
    BUDDY.
WELL THEY ARE.
    TERRY.
LET'S GIVE THEM FLOWERS

BUDDY.
THAT'S GOING TOO FAR
TERRY. Why?
BUDDY.
FLOWERS ARE ROMANTIC
ROMANCE IS IN THE AIR
SO BEWARE
TERRY. You've got so much to learn.
YOU DON'T KNOW WOMEN

LET ME SET YOU RIGHT

THEY'LL TRY TO HOOK YOU

BUT YOU DON'T HAVE TO
  BITE
I'VE KNOWN LOTS OF
  WOMEN

BUDDY.
NOT LIKE THEM

I KNOW MORE THAN YOU
  THINK

Oh come on.

SO I'VE HEARD

TERRY.
THE LOVELY
THE GRUESOME
I'VE SEEN THINGS
I'VE TRIED THINGS
BUT NEVER A TWOSOME!
BUDDY.
I'M NOT INTERESTED IN THAT
TERRY.
THEN CLOSE YOUR EYES
BUDDY. What?
TERRY.
JUST A LITTLE JOKE
BUDDY.
IT'S NO JOKING MATTER
TERRY.
YOU WORRY TOO MUCH
BUDDY.   **TERRY.**
I'M JUST SAYING WE NEED
  TO LOOK

LOOK AT WHAT?

LOOK AT WHERE THIS ROAD
  LEADS

BUDDY. (Cont.)

IT'S NOT RIGHT WE OVERLOOK
THEIR NEEDS
THEY HAVE NEEDS

ARE WE DOING WHAT'S FAIR
  AND RIGHT?

WISH I COULD KNOW WHAT'S
  IN STORE

TERRY. (Cont.)
TO VAUDEVILLE

WE'RE GIVING THEM
  THE CHANCE OF A
  LIFETIME

YES WE ARE

WHO KNOWS THAT?

TERRY and BUDDY.
THE FUTURE SHOULD BE CLEAR TONIGHT

BUDDY.
I THINK WE'RE GETTING MORE

TERRY.
ARE WE GETTING MORE

TERRY and BUDDY.
THAN WE BARGAINED FOR
THAN WE BARGAINED FOR
THAN WE BARGAINED FOR

*(ROUSTABOUTS help readjust the set to create dressing area for
    DAISY and VIOLET.)*

Scene 5 - IN THE DRESSING AREA

*(The FORTUNE TELLER and JAKE are helping DAISY and VIO-
    LET get ready for their performance.)*

(#8 "Side Show's About to Explode")

FORTUNE TELLER.
SIDESHOW'S ABOUT TO EXPLODE WITH EXCITEMENT
EVERYONE'S HEADING FOR THE TENT
THEY'VE HEARD ABOUT
THE HOURS YOU'VE SPENT
LEARNING YOUR SONG

JAKE.
I HOPE NOTHING GOES WRONG

FORTUNE TELLER.
DON'T WORRY, JAKE
THEIR FUTURE LOOKS ROSY
I SEE BOTH OF YOU
FALLING IN LOVE

(TERRY and BUDDY enter, each holding flowers behind his back.)

TERRY.
CONGRATULATIONS
BUDDY.
WHAT AN OCCASION
TERRY.
THE HILTON SISTERS' DEBUT!

(TERRY presents flowers to DAISY. BUDDY gives his bouquet to VIOLET.)

DAISY.
FLOWERS?
VIOLET.
FOR US?
FORTUNE TELLER.
HOW THOUGHTFUL
TERRY.
WE'RE ALL PULLING FOR YOUR SUCCESS
JAKE. You should be getting dressed.
VIOLET.
THANK YOU ALL
FOR ALL YOUR HELP
FORTUNE TELLER.
WE'D BETTER GO
WE'LL BE IN THE FRONT ROW
JAKE.
ROOTING FOR YOU ALL THE WAY

(JAKE and FORTUNE TELLER exit.)

TERRY.
YOUR FRIENDS CAN'T WAIT
TO HEAR YOU SING
BUDDY.
AND I'M SO PROUD
I HOPE YOU KNOW

TERRY and BUDDY.
HERE'S TO A WONDERFUL SHOW

(TERRY and BUDDY exit.)

(#8A "Feelings You Have Got to Hide")

DAISY.
ALL OF OUR DREAMS
ARE COMING TRUE
VIOLET.
AT LEAST THE DREAM
THAT'S STARRING YOU
DAISY.
TERRY'S MY DREAM PERSONIFIED
I CAN FEEL HIM THERE
RIGHT BY MY SIDE
I CAN FEEL HIS LOVE
I CAN FEEL HIS PRIDE
VIOLET.
THOSE ARE FEELINGS
YOU HAVE GOT TO HIDE
DAISY.
WHY DO I FEEL
LIKE I SWALLOWED A BUTTERFLY?
TICKLING INSIDE
MAKES ME LAUGH
TILL I WANT TO CRY
WHY ARE MY EYES TURNING MOIST
WHILE MY THROAT IS DRY?
IS IT THAT HANDSOME GUY?

WHY ARE MY FEELINGS
RACING AROUND INSIDE?
WILL I EXPLODE
IF ALL OF MY THOUGHTS COLLIDE?
ONE MINUTE BRAVE
THE NEXT MINUTE TERRIFIED
ARE THESE FEELINGS I HAVE GOT TO HIDE?
VIOLET.
DON'T LET YOUR HEART
LEAD YOUR HEAD ASTRAY
HE COULDN'T POSSIBLY FEEL THAT WAY

DAISY.
I KNOW HE LOVES ME
I KNOW I'LL BE HIS BRIDE
   VIOLET.
THOSE ARE FEELINGS YOU HAVE GOT TO HIDE

DO NOT TELL
DO NOT CONFIDE
THESE LONGINGS CAN'T BE SATISFIED
THIS WAVE WILL WASH OUT WITH THE TIDE
THESE ARE FEELINGS YOU'VE GOT TO HIDE
   DAISY.
I CAN'T HIDE WHAT I FEEL
THE WAY THAT YOU DO
   VIOLET.
WHAT DO YOU MEAN?
I'M NOT IN LOVE LIKE YOU
   DAISY.
I THINK YOU ARE
AND BUDDY IS THE GUY
   VIOLET.
WHY DO YOU SAY THAT
TELL ME WHY
   DAISY.
I'M YOUR SISTER
I'M YOUR SHADOW
I DO KNOW
   VIOLET.
OH YOU KNOW ... ?
   DAISY.
YES I KNOW
   VIOLET.
WHAT I'M THINKING
   DAISY.
WHAT YOU'RE THINKING
I'M NOT DEAF
I'M NOT BLIND
   VIOLET.
YOU CAN ALWAYS ...
   DAISY.   **VIOLET.**
READ YOUR MIND   READ MY MIND

VIOLET.
NOW I'M THE ONE
LIGHTING UP LIKE A FIREFLY
NOW I'M THE ONE
BLUSHING RED
EATING HUMBLE PIE
WHY DO I WANT TO TELL ALL
AND YET FEEL SO SHY
ABOUT THAT HANDSOME GUY
    DAISY.
YOU WANT A HUSBAND
YOU WANT TO BE A BRIDE
    VIOLET.
HEART IN MY THROAT
LIKE I'M ON A MIDWAY RIDE
BUT I'LL NEVER SHOW
WHAT'S GOING ON INSIDE
THESE ARE FEELINGS YOU'VE GOT TO HIDE
    DAISY.
WHY DO YOU FEEL THAT WAY?
    VIOLET.
FEELINGS AREN'T FOR DISPLAY
    DAISY.
LET'S ANNOUNCE LOVE TODAY!
    VIOLET.
YOU WOULD SHOUT
WHAT YOU SHOULD NEVER SAY
    DAISY.
WHY ARE THESE FEELINGS
RACING AROUND INSIDE?

WILL ALL MY THOUGHTS
  COLLIDE?

I KNOW I'LL BE HIS BRIDE

ARE THESE
FEELINGS I'VE GOT TO HIDE

    VIOLET.
THESE LONGINGS CAN'T
  BE SATISFIED

THIS WAVE WILL WASH
  OUT WITH THE TIDE

THESE ARE FEELINGS
  YOU'VE GOT TO HIDE

FEELINGS YOU'VE GOT
  TO HIDE

(On applause, DAISY and VIOLET exit as ROUSTABOUTS help
change the set to inside the tent position.)

Scene 6 - IN THE TENT

(The ATTRACTIONS, wearing robes and sleepwear, tiptoe in and
take their seats for the performance.)

(#9 "Ladies and Gentlemen, Glad you Came")

BUDDY.
LADIES AND GENTLEMEN
GLAD YOU CAME
THOUGH IT'S LATE
YOU WON'T REGRET THE EFFORT YOU MADE
THE SLEEP THAT IS LOST
IS ALL YOU'VE PAID
TOMORROW YOU'RE LEAVING
GOING AWAY FROM HERE
ONLY HAVE TONIGHT
TO OFFER THE TWINS PREMIERE
REMEMBER THIS SECRET SHOW
WHEN YOU THINK OF SAN ANTONIO
    Ladies and gentlemen, I give you—two of your own—Daisy and
Violet Hilton!

(#9A "When I'm By Your Side")

DAISY and VIOLET.
YOU ARE MY FAV'RITE NEW PLAYMATE
I LOVE THE FUN YOU PROVIDE
A SONG AND A LAUGH
ARE BETTER BY HALF
WHEN I'M BY YOUR SIDE

HAPPY TO BE YOUR COMPANION
GLAD THAT I QUALIFIED
I FEEL AS GRAND AS THE CANYON
WHEN I'M BY YOUR SIDE

DAISY and VIOLET. (Cont.)
PEOPLE STOP DEAD WHEN THEY'VE SEEN US
WE TAKE THEIR STARING IN STRIDE
CAN'T FIT A NEEDLE BETWEEN US
WHEN I'M BY YOUR SIDE

WE'RE AN UNUSUAL DUO
DON'T ALWAYS SWIM WITH THE TIDE
BUT WHO NEEDS A BOAT
I'M ALWAYS AFLOAT
WHEN I'M BY YOUR SIDE

(Dance)

I LIKE WHAT A DUO CAN DO
THE COMBINATION IS GREATER
THAN THE SUM OF ITS PARTS

SHOULD WE CEMENT THIS ARRANGEMENT?
NOW THAT IT'S TESTED AND TRIED
WE'RE SUCH A TIGHT WEAVE
I DON'T WANT TO LEAVE
WE MAKE A MATCHED SET
A PERFECT DUET
LIKE EGGS ARE TO HAM
LIKE TWINS TO SIAM
I'M BY YOUR SIDE
     THE BOSS. *(Entering.)* What the hell is all this racket? You two.
I might have known. What are you doing here?

(#9B "They Came to Hear Us Sing")

DAISY.
THEY CAME TO HEAR US SING
     THE BOSS. Sing?
     VIOLET.
WE CAN SING
WE DID SING
     THE BOSS. You girls get back to your trailer.
     DAISY.
DON'T TELL US WHAT TO DO
     THE BOSS. You're asking for it.

VIOLET.
WE'RE NOT ASKING FOR ANYTHING
DAISY.
WE'RE LEAVING THE SIDESHOW
THE BOSS. *(Starts to remove his belt.)* We'll just see about that. *(JAKE steps between THE BOSS and the TWINS.)* Out of the way, Jake. Jake, get out of my way or get out of the sideshow. Have you all lost your minds? I'll fire the lot of you.
JAKE. And put yourself on display?

(The ATTRACTIONS start to laugh, building to an uproar.)

THE BOSS. This is the thanks I get? Giving you shelter and food in this Depression?
ATTRACTION.
SHELTER?
ATTRACTION.
RAMSHACKLE TRAILERS
ATTRACTION.
FOOD?
ATTRACTION.
STALE BREAD AND SLOP
ATTRACTION.
AND YOU CHARGE US FOR THOSE
TAKE IT OUT OF OUR PAY
THE BOSS. I give you jobs!

(The ATTRACTIONS surround THE BOSS.)

ATTRACTION.
WE DO OUR JOBS
YOU TAKE THE GATE
ATTRACTION.
WE HOLD OUR TONGUES
ATTRACTION.
WHILE YOU BERATE AND SCOLD
ATTRACTION.
AND TREAT US WRONG
ALL.
WE'VE HAD ENOUGH
WE WON'T GO ON
YOU'D BETTER CHANGE OR WE'LL BE GONE
AND LEAVE YOU HIGH AND DRY

ATTRACTION.
OR DO YOU WANT TO SAY GOOD-BYE?
ALL.
SAY GOOD-BYE TO THE FREAK SHOW?
TO YOUR SINGULAR SOURCE OF DOUGH?
IF YOU PUSH TOO HARD
OR YOU HIT TOO LOW
SAY GOOD-BYE TO THE FREAK SHOW
GOOD-BYE
THE BOSS.
I'VE SPENT A LIFETIME IN SIDESHOWS
I CAN SPOT A CON A MILE AWAY
WHEN THAT SNAKE IN A SUIT
SHEDS HIS SKIN
ALL THEY'LL HAVE IS HELL TO PAY

I'M ONE OF YOU
AND NOW OUR ENTERPRISE
IS LESS THAN BEFORE
SO WE NEED EACH OTHER MORE

DOWN THE ROAD
WE'VE GOT A SHOW TO DO
TOMORROW WE PLAY A NEW SITE
ALL OF US COULD USE SOME REST
SO I WILL SAY GOOD NIGHT

(THE BOSS exits.)

VIOLET.
WHAT HAVE WE DONE?
DAISY.
LOST OUR JOBS
VIOLET.
CLOSED A DOOR
TERRY.
OPENED MORE!
MY BEAUTIES, MY LOVES
I CAN SEE US FLOATING TO THE STARS
IN A MAGIC BOAT
PROPELLED BY YOUR TALENT
AND UNPARALLELED BEAUTY

DAISY.
ALL BECAUSE OF YOU
VIOLET.
ALL WE'VE EVER KNOWN IS THE MID-WAY
TERRY.
WAIT TILL YOU SEE
YOUR NAMES ON THE MARQUEE
ALL THE WAY FROM FRISCO TO DALLAS
SOME DAY YOU WILL PLAY THE PALACE
VIOLET.
WE'RE NOT THAT GOOD
DAISY.
WE COULD BE
WITH YOU BEHIND US
BUDDY.
DON'T YOU FRET
WE'RE WITH YOU HEART AND SOUL
TERRY.
YOUR SWEET DUET
IS OUR ACE IN THE HOLE
BUDDY.
NOW WILL YOU GIVE YOUR ALL FOR OUR GOAL?
VIOLET.
OH YES—WE'LL DO OUR BEST
TERRY.
I KNOW YOU WILL
AND YOUR BEST WILL GO FAR
YOUR TALENT'S THE KEY
NOW THE DOOR IS AJAR
YOU WILL FRAME THE MOONLIGHT
EACH A SHINING STAR

(#10 "Say Good-bye to the Freakshow")

TERRY. (Cont.)
SAY GOOD-BYE TO THE FREAK SHOW
SAY HELLO TO THE FOOTLIGHT'S GLOW
YOUR SUCCESS CAN ONLY GROW
SAY GOOD-BYE TO THE FREAK SHOW
ATTRACTIONS.
GOOD-BYE
DAISY.
GOOD-BYE

DAISY. (Cont.)
WE WILL MISS YOU
  GEEK.
DON'T CRY
LET ME KISS YOU
  VIOLET.
OH MY
WHY SHOULD IT BE SO HARD
TO SAY GOOD-BYE
  HAREM GIRL 1.
FAREWELL
DON'T FORGET US
  BEARDED LADY.
DO TELL HOW YOU MET US
  6TH EXHIBIT.
DON'T DWELL ON SORROW AS YOU GO
  DOLLY.
YOU WILL FARE WELL
  FORTUNE TELLER.
NOW, NOW
SAYING GOOD-BYE IS PART OF GROWING UP
THERE'S A WHOLE NEW WORLD
OF FRIENDS FOR YOU TO MAKE
  JAKE.
GOOD-BYE, DAISY
DEAR, SWEET VIOLET
  DAISY and VIOLET.
OH NO!
NOT GOOD-BYE TO JAKE
  JAKE.
TAKE WING
FLY TO GLORY
DANCE, SING
TELL YOUR STORY
YOU BRING SUCH JOY
TO THOSE YOU'VE KNOWN
TAKE FLIGHT, TAKE WING
  TERRY.
JAKE, LOOKS LIKE THEIR HEARTS MIGHT BREAK
SAYING GOOD-BYE TO YOU
YOU'RE A FRIEND TO THE TWINS
YOU'VE HELPED THEM ALONG
CONSTANT SUPPORT

TERRY. (Cont.)
QUIET AND STRONG
WE COULD USE YOU BACKSTAGE
AS WE TOUR WITH THEIR ACT
WHY NOT JOIN THE TROUPE
YOUR BAG IS PACKED
  DAISY.
YES—SAY YES
  VIOLET.
PLEASE COME ALONG
  JAKE.
NOTHING LOST IF I DECIDE TO
I FEEL I BELONG BESIDE YOU
  ATTRACTIONS.
SAY GOOD-BYE TO THE FREAK SHOW
BLESS YOUR NEW IMPRESARIO
WE ALWAYS KNEW YOU WOULD OUTGROW
THE TENTS OF THE SIDESHOW
GOOD-BYE

(The ROUSTABOUTS start striking the sideshow set as the ATTRAC-
TIONS form a tableau Upstage.)

  ATTRACTIONS. (Cont.)
STRIKE TENTS
PULL THE STAKES UP
GO GENTS
LET THE BRAKES UP
NO FENCE
STOPS US FROM MOVING ON
TO OUR NEXT SHOW

FAREWELL
DON'T FORGET US
DO TELL HOW YOU MET US
DON'T DWELL ON SORROW AS YOU GO
YOU WILL FARE WELL
GOOD-BYE

(DAISY and VIOLET wave good-bye to the ATTRACTIONS. Then
TERRY leads them Offstage with BUDDY and JAKE following.)

Scene 7 - VAUDEVILLE - PRESS CONFERENCE

(TERRY addresses a group of rowdy MALE REPORTERS.)

(#11 "The Press Conference")

TERRY.
THANK YOU, MY FRIENDS
FROM THE FOURTH ESTATE
FOR COMING TONIGHT
    REPORTER 1.
THIS BETTER BE GOOD
BECAUSE VAUDEVILLE IS FADING
    REPORTER 2.
OUR READERS HAVE MORE INTEREST
IN PICTURES THAT TALK
    REPORTER 3.
GIVE THE MAN A CHANCE, GUYS
HE ALWAYS COMES THROUGH
    REPORTER 4.
HIS STORIES ARE GREAT
AND SOME OF THEM ARE TRUE
    TERRY.
HAVE I EVER LIED TO YOU?
    REPORTERS.
WELL, MAYBE NOT LIED
EXAGGERATED HERE AND THERE
    TERRY.
I'M GIVING YOU THE CHANCE
TO JUMP THE GUN
AND RUN THE STORY
IN YOUR PUBLICATIONS
OF THESE DOUBLE-DUTY SENSATIONS
    REPORTER 5. Double-duty?
    REPORTER 6. What the hell are they?
    TERRY.
THEY ARE DAISY AND VIOLET HILTON
THE MOST TALENTED, LOVELY
AND CHARMING OF HEROINES
WHO HAPPEN TO BE SIAMESE TWINS

REPORTER 7. Siamese twins?
REPORTER 8.
TERRY, HAVE YOU SUNK SO LOW
YOU NEED CLIENTS FROM THE FREAK SHOW?
TERRY.
NO, NO, NO

MY CLIENTS WILL BE AN OVERNIGHT SENSATION
WAIT TILL YOU SEE THEM ON STAGE
WAIT TILL YOUR DOUBT
TURNS INTO FASCINATION
THEIR STORY WILL LEAP OFF THE PAGE
YOU'LL ENGAGE
IN MANIC SPECULATION
ABOUT THIS OVERNIGHT SENSATION

(TERRY and REPORTERS exit. Upstage, DAISY and VIOLET are revealed with BUDDY posing them for a Photographer.)

Scene 8 - PHOTO SHOOT

(#11 "The Photo Shoot")

BUDDY.
VIOLET
DON'T BE AFRAID OF THE CAMERA
JUST RELAX
VIOLET.
I DON'T KNOW HOW
BUDDY.
LOOK INTO THE CAMERA
LIKE YOU'RE LOOKING IN THE EYES
OF THE ONE YOU LOVE
DAISY.
THAT SHOULDN'T BE TOO HARD
VIOLET.
WATCH IT, DAISY
DAISY.
I LOVE THE CAMERA

DAISY. (Cont.)
I FEEL LIKE A MOVIE STAR

(TERRY enters.)

DAISY. (Cont.) What do you think, Terry?
COULD I BE A GODDESS
OF THE SILVER SCREEN?
  TERRY.
AFTER TONIGHT
THE WORLD'S YOUR OYSTER

YOU'RE GONNA BE AN OVERNIGHT SENSATION
I BROUGHT THE PRESS AND THEY'RE PRIMED
TALK OF THE TOWN
THEN TALK OF THE NATION
AFTER THE HURDLES WE'VE CLIMBED
WE HAVE TIMED THIS EVENING'S PRESENTATION
TO MAKE AN OVERNIGHT SENSATION

Scene 9 - BACKSTAGE

(BUDDY and TERRY escort DAISY and VIOLET Downstage.)

(#11, cont. "Backstage Before the Show")

  BUDDY.
AND AFTER YOUR ACT TONIGHT
WHEN YOUR INTERVIEW'S THROUGH
WE'VE GOT A SURPRISE
A ROOM WITH A VIEW
  TERRY.
TO TOAST OUR TRIUMPHANT TWO
THE FINEST HOTEL
  BUDDY.
IT'LL BE SWELL
LIKE YOU
  TERRY.
YOU'RE GONNA BE AN OVERNIGHT

BUDDY.
OVERNIGHT
TERRY and BUDDY.
YOU'RE GONNA BE AN OVERNIGHT SENSATION
BUDDY. See you out there.

(BUDDY exits.)

(#12 "Leave Me Alone")

DAISY.
TERRY, HOW ABOUT A GOOD LUCK KISS?
TERRY.
WELL-DESERVED
BREAK A LEG
HAVE FUN
DAISY.
I ALWAYS HAVE FUN
WHEN YOU'RE AROUND
TERRY.
LIKEWISE
YOU'RE A GOOD-TIME GIRL

(TERRY exits.)

VIOLET.
YOU ARE SHAMELESS
A SHAMELESS FLIRT
DAISY.
SHOWING SOME INTEREST
COULDN'T HURT
VIOLET.
SOME?
YOU SHOW THE MAXIMUM!
DAISY.
AND YOU'D PREFER
I ACT LIKE YOU?
AFRAID TO SHOW INTEREST
AFRAID IT'S TABOO
HOW WILL YOUR BUDDY
EVER HAVE A CLUE
THAT YOU LOVE HIM THROUGH AND THROUGH?

VIOLET.
DON'T SAY THAT!
HE MIGHT OVERHEAR
  DAISY.
SO WHAT
WHY LIVE IN FEAR?
HE MIGHT FEEL THE SAME
BUT HE'S SHY
  VIOLET.
SO AM I
I DESPISE
THE WAY YOU ADVERTISE
  DAISY.
I HATE
YOUR COY LITTLE ACT
  VIOLET.
IS THAT A FACT?
  DAISY.
LEAVE ME ALONE
THIS IS NONE OF YOUR BUSINESS
YOU DON'T NEED TO JUDGE
OR OFFER ADVICE
YOU'RE NOT MY MOTHER
YOU'RE NOT MY WARDEN
DON'T NEED A STRICT CHAPERONE
WHY DON'T YOU LEAVE ME ALONE
  VIOLET.
LEAVE YOU ALONE?
I AM TRYING TO HELP YOU
YOUR BLATANT BEHAVIOR
EMBARRASSES ME
IF YOU COULD SEE YOU
FROM MY PERSPECTIVE
YOU WOULDN'T LIKE WHAT YOU WERE SHOWN
NO I WON'T LEAVE YOU ALONE
  DAISY.

DAISY.	VIOLET.
LEAVE ME ALONE	**VIOLET.**
	AND HOW WOULD I DO THAT?
LEAVE ME ALONE	
	TELL ME WHERE WOULD I GO?
LEAVE ME ALONE	
	BELIEVE ME I'D LOVE TO
I NEED SOME TIME ON MY OWN	

DAISY. (Cont.)	VIOLET. (Cont.)
LEAVE ME ALONE	LEAVE YOU ALONE?
YOU DON'T KNOW	CAN YOU HEAR
WHAT YOU'RE SAYING	WHAT YOU'RE SAYING?
YOU'LL NEVER FIND LOVE	YOU WON'T FIND LOVE
BY PLAYING IT SHY	BY CHASING THE GUY
DON'T NEED THE WISDOM	I DON'T HAVE WISDOM
OR THE OPINION	JUST AN OPINION
YOU GRANDLY DISPENSE	
FROM YOUR THRONE	MY THRONE? OH NO
WHY DON'T YOU LEAVE	
ME ALONE?	I WON'T
	LEAVE YOU ALONE?
THAT'S WHAT I'M ASKING	
	LEAVE YOU ALONE?
IT'S A SIMPLE REQUEST	
	LEAVE YOU ALONE?
I'D BE FINE WITHOUT YOU	
I NEED SOME TIME ON MY	
OWN	
	I DON'T LIKE YOUR TONE
WHY DON'T YOU	
	HOW COULD I
I HATE YOU	
	SO DO I
WHY	WHY
DON'T YOU LEAVE ME	DON'T YOU LEAVE ME
ALONE?!	ALONE?!

(DAISY and VIOLET exit Upstage as the ROUSTABOUTS, costumed in safari gear, enter as ARCHEOLOGISTS.)

Scene 10 - ONSTAGE

(#13 "We Share Everything" Part 1)

4 ARCHEOLOGISTS.
WE'VE TRAVELED FROM NOME TO BALI
SEEN THE HIST'RY OF HUMAN FOLLY

4 ARCHEOLOGISTS. (Cont.)
COURTED DANGER TILL OUR HAIR WAS CURLED
SEEN ALL SEVEN WONDERS OF THE WORLD

THOSE WONDERS HAVE MOSTLY CRUMBLED
BUILT BY PEOPLE, DOWN THEY TUMBLED
WONDERS MADE BY NATURE NEVER RUST
BUT THOSE MADE BY HUMANS TURN TO DUST

WHILE THOSE SEVEN WONDERS DETERIORATE
OUR NEW DISCOVERY IS RIGHT UP TO DATE
THIS IS A WONDER YOU CAN'T DUPLICATE
CLEAN THE SLATE
HERE'S THE GREAT NUMBER EIGHT

(The ARCHEOLOGISTS approach a tomb covered with hieroglyphics. They pull open the doors to reveal DAISY and VIOLET as Egyptian royalty. ARCHEOLOGISTS exit.)

(#13A "We Share Everything" Part 2)

DAISY and VIOLET.
LIFE'S DUCKY
BALMY WEATHER
WE'RE LUCKY
WE'RE TOGETHER
WE'RE A PAIR REMARKABLY MATED
PEOPLE SWEAR WE MUST BE RELATED
WE CAN'T BEAR TO BE SEPARATED
WE SHARE EVERYTHING

TWO SONGBIRDS
ZERO FRICTION
NO STRONG WORDS
DAINTY DICTION
HARMONY IS WHAT WE ALWAYS SING
WE'RE SO HAPPY
WE SHARE EVERYTHING

AIN'T IT AMAZING
EVEN OUR PHRASING
SOUNDS LIKE IT'S COMING FROM ONE

DAISY and VIOLET. (Cont.)
NOBODY'S SWEATING
WHEN WE'RE DUETTING
CAUSE WE'RE HAVIN' SUCH FUN
EVEN MORE WHEN WE GO DANCIN'
   DAISY.
YOU SHOULD HEAR THE ROAR
   VIOLET.
WHEN WE HIT THE FLOOR
   DAISY.
WE'RE SO CLOSELY MATCHED
   VIOLET.
NEVER UNATTACHED
   DAISY and VIOLET.
LIFE'S BREEZY
NO DISSENSION
LIFE'S EASY
WITHOUT TENSION
WE'RE LIKE BEES
WHO NEVER NEED TO STING
WE'RE SO HAPPY
SHARING THE HONEY
WE'RE SO HAPPY
SHARING OUR MONEY
WE'RE SO HAPPY
WE SHARE EVERYTHING

(Dance break.)

   DAISY and VIOLET. (Cont.)
WE'RE SO HAPPY
WE SHARE EVERYTHING
   VIOLET.
NEVER DIVISION
ON ANY DECISION
NEVER A WORD THAT'S SEVERE
   DAISY.
TWO DIFFERENT VOICES
IDENTICAL CHOICES
NEVER AN ARGUMENT HERE
   DAISY and VIOLET.
WE'RE BOTH SWEET AND UNDERSTANDING

WE DIVIDE THE PIE
WE SEE EYE-TO-EYE

WE'RE NEVER PUSHY-SHOVEY
FOREVER LOVEY-DOVEY
ALL THROUGH SUMMER
WINTER, FALL OR SPRING
WE'RE UNITED THROUGH EVERY SEASON
WE'RE DELIGHTED
YOU KNOW THE REASON
YOU CAN SHARE TOO
THERE'S NOTHING TO IT
SO PREPARE TO
WATCH HOW WE DO IT

(EIGHT PHARAOHS enter and dance with DAISY and VIOLET.)

    PHARAOHS.
EVEN MORE WHEN WE GO DANCING
    DAISY and VIOLET.
YOU SHOULD HEAR THE ROAR
WHEN WE HIT THE FLOOR

AYE-YI-YI-YI
AYE-YI-YI-YI-YI-YI-YI!
    Come on, boys
    Build a barge
    Make it fancy
    Make it large
    Grab an oar
    Row with style
    Take us down the Nile!

(The PHARAOHS create a barge and, grabbing oars, "row" DAISY and VIOLET down the Nile.)

    DAISY and VIOLET. (Cont.)
WE'RE SO HAPPY
WE SHARE EVERYTHING
    PHARAOHS.
WE'RE SO HAPPY
WE'RE SO HAPPY
WE'RE SO HAPPY

ALL.
WE SHARE EVERYTHING

*(End of song. Then playoff music as PHARAOHS "row" barge Off-
stage.)*

PHARAOHS.
WE'RE SO HAPPY
WE'RE SO HAPPY
WE'RE SO HAPPY
WE'RE SO HAPPY
WE'RE SO HAPPY
WE'RE SO HAPPY
   DAISY and VIOLET.
WE SHARE EVERYTHING

(#13 "Scene Change")

Scene 11 - BACKSTAGE

*(A REPORTER and PHOTOGRAPHER enter and head toward the
outside of the HILTON's dressing room. JAKE enters and shoos
the Press People away. BUDDY enters.)*

(#14 "I Knew They Were Meant to Sing")

BUDDY.
I KNEW THEY WERE MEANT TO SING
BUT TONIGHT THEY DID MORE
   JAKE.
DID YOU HEAR THAT CROWD?
THEY HOLLERED SO LOUD
I BET THEIR THROATS ARE SORE
   BUDDY.
THIS ISN'T A DREAM
DID YOU HEAR THEM SCREAM ENCORE!

(BUDDY and JAKE cross to DAISY and VIOLET, who are revealed, no longer wearing their Egyptian costumes.)

BUDDY and JAKE.
YOU'RE GONNA BE AN OVERNIGHT

(TERRY enters.)

TERRY.
OVERNIGHT!
JAKE, TERRY, BUDDY.
YOU'RE GONNA BE AN OVERNIGHT SENSATION!
TERRY.
MAGNIFICENT!

(TERRY kisses DAISY.)

BUDDY.
WONDERFUL!
VIOLET.
I ACTUALLY ENJOYED MYSELF
BUDDY.
OH, VIOLET, I'M SO HAPPY TO HEAR THAT

(BUDDY kisses VIOLET.)

DAISY.
IF WE ALWAYS GET KISSES
I'LL TRY EVEN HARDER
TERRY.
KISSES ARE A TINY REWARD
VIOLET.
NOT FOR US
BUDDY.
THEN GET READY FOR ANOTHER
TERRY.
AND ANOTHER
BUDDY.
AND ANOTHER
TERRY and BUDDY.
HERE'S TO A WONDERFUL SHOW

(TERRY ushers REPORTERS into the area.)

REPORTERS and PHOTOGRAPHERS.
WHEN CAN WE MEET THIS OVERNIGHT SENSATION?
WHEN CAN WE TALK TO THE STARS?
WE WANT THE FACTS WITHOUT EXAGGERATION
THIS STORY WILL WIN US CIGARS
CERTAIN BARS AWAIT OUR VISITATION
TO TOAST THIS OVERNIGHT SENSATION
   TERRY. Gentlemen, the Hilton Sisters!

(#14A "The Interview")

   ALL REPORTERS.
WE'VE GOT A MILLION QUESTIONS FOR YOU
   REPORTER 1.
WOULD YOU START BY REMINDING US
WHICH ONE IS WHO?
   DAISY.
I'M DAISY.
   VIOLET.
I'M VIOLET.
   DAISY and VIOLET.
WE'RE SIAMESE TWINS
   VIOLET.
I'M TO YOUR RIGHT
AS YOU WATCH OUR SHOW
   DAISY.
SHE THINKS SHE'S ALWAYS RIGHT
NOT SO
I'M DAISY
   VIOLET.
I'M VIOLET
   DAISY and VIOLET.
WHAT ELSE WOULD YOU LIKE TO KNOW?
   REPORTER 2.
COULD YOU BE SEPARATED?
   REPORTER 3.
HAVE DOCTORS EXAMINED YOU?
   DAISY.
IN HUNDREDS OF WAYS
   VIOLET.
FROM OUR EARLIEST DAYS
   DAISY.
SOME THINK WE COULD BE SEPARATED

VIOLET.
SOME WOULD LOVE TO TRY
DAISY and VIOLET.
SOME THINK WE WOULD DIE
REPORTER 2.
HOW DO YOU SLEEP?
DAISY and VIOLET.
IN A BED
REPORTER 4.
BUT DOES ONE
EVER KEEP THE OTHER AWAKE?
DAISY.
WELL, IT DOES TAKE A BIT OF DOING
VIOLET.
IF ONE OF US WANTS TO ROLL OVER
DAISY and VIOLET.
BUT WHOSE LIFE IS A BED OF CLOVER?
TERRY.
CERTAINLY NOT YOURS
REPORTER 1.
WHAT ABOUT ROMANCE?
REPORTER 5.
WHAT ABOUT LOVE?
REPORTER 6.
WHAT ABOUT BEAUX?
VIOLET.
OH THOSE
I SUPPOSE
IT'S BOUND TO HAPPEN
DAISY.
SOME DAY
VIOLET.
SOME NIGHT
WHEN THE MOON
IS JUST RIGHT
DAISY.
WHEN THE UNIVERSE HUMS
VIOLET.
WHEN THE GUY COMES ALONG
WHO HEARS THE SINGER
MORE THAN THE SONG
DAISY.
SOME DAY

VIOLET.
SOME NIGHT
DAISY and VIOLET.
LOVE WILL FEEL RIGHT

(Lights change to indicate DAISY and VIOLET's inner thoughts, as REPORTERS mime asking questions in slow motion.)

VIOLET.
BUDDY KISSED ME
HE KISSED ME
FOR THE FIRST TIME
DAISY.
I FORCED A KISS
BEFORE THE SHOW
BUT NOT THE KISSES THAT FOLLOWED
VIOLET.
YOUR LIPS PROVE WE'RE SHARING
THE WARMTH THAT I FELT
THE FROST ON MY HEART
IS BEGINNING TO MELT
DAISY.
YOU CAN'T MINIMIZE
ALL THE HEAT IN YOUR EYES
YOUR PASSION IS NOT A SURPRISE

(Light change indicating DAISY and VIOLET are back in real time.)

REPORTER 6.
YOU'RE WORKING WITH SEVERAL MEN
REPORTER 7.
LIKE TERRY
REPORTER 3.
THAT FOSTER KID
REPORTER 6.
THE COLORED GUY
REPORTER 4.
HOW CLOSE ARE ALL OF YOU?
REPORTER 8.
VERY CLOSE?
VIOLET.
WE WOULDN'T BE HERE
WITHOUT THEIR HELP

DAISY.
WE SHARE THE APPLAUSE WITH THEM
   REPORTER 6.
ANYTHING ELSE?
   REPORTER 1.
YOUR ROOM?
   REPORTER 6.
YOUR BED?
   JAKE. Watch your mouth, Mister.
   TERRY.
NOT TO THROW COLD WATER
ON YOUR SICK FANTASIZING
BUT THIS IS BUSINESS
NO ROMANCE INVOLVED
   BUDDY.
WE'D NEVER TAKE ADVANTAGE
OF THESE GIRLS
   TERRY.
THE SUGGESTION IS ABSURD
I HAVE A SWEETHEART AT HOME
   REPORTER 4.
NOT ONLY THERE SO I'VE HEARD
   REPORTER 7.
SO NONE OF YOU HAS INTEREST
IN A DOUBLE-HEADER?
   JAKE. No one talks to them that way!
   TERRY. All right, Jake. I'll handle this.

*(Again lights change to indicate DAISY and VIOLET's inner
   thoughts.)*

   VIOLET.
I'M NOT REALLY HERE
NOTHING THEY'RE SAYING
IS CATCHING MY EAR
AND I'M VIRTUALLY BLIND
NO MORE ROOM IN MY MIND
HE KISSED ME
   DAISY.
ONE MINUTE BLISS
BECAUSE OF HIS KISS
THEN CRIPPLING DOUBT

DAISY. (Cont.)
WHEN THE TRUTH COMES OUT
ALL THAT I FELT WAS A LIE

                                    VIOLET.
    DAISY.   I FELT LOVE WITHIN YOU
HOW CAN WE CONTINUE?

                                 THE SEEDS WE HAVE
                                     PLANTED WILL BLOOM

ENOUGH OF THESE QUESTIONS

                                 I CAN'T HEAR THE QUESTIONS
    DAISY and VIOLET.
I CAN'T KEEP MY MIND IN THE ROOM

(Lights change to indicate DAISY and VIOLET are back in real time.)

    REPORTER 6.
DON'T YOU NEED A MAN?
    REPORTER 3.
DON'T YOU WANT TO GET MARRIED?
    REPORTERS 1 & 7.
HUSBANDS?
    REPORTERS 2,3 & 6.
CHILDREN?
    REPORTERS 1,4,5,6 & 8.
FAM'LIES?
    REPORTER 8.
DON'T YOU FEEL LIKE NUNS?
    REPORTER 6.
WILL YOU ALWAYS BE VIRGINS?
    REPORTERS 1,2,3 & 7.
OLD MAIDS?
    REPORTERS 4,5,6 & 8.
SPINSTERS?
    ALL REPORTERS.
BARREN?
    VIOLET.
LIKE ANY GIRLS OUR AGE
WE DREAM OF GETTING MARRIED
A WEDDING
    DAISY.
A HUSBAND
    VIOLET.
A FAM'LY TO COME HOME TO

FOUR REPORTERS.
HOW WOULD THAT WORK?

                              FOUR REPORTERS.
                              HOW WOULD THAT WORK?

ALL REPORTERS.
WITH YOUR CONDITION?
DAISY.
ANYTHING'S POSSIBLE
VIOLET.
WHEN EVERYTHING'S RIGHT
DAISY.
I'M DAISY
VIOLET.
I'M VIOLET
TERRY.
GOOD NIGHT

(Grumbling, the REPORTERS exit followed by JAKE, BUDDY & TERRY.)

(#14B "Buddy Kissed Me")

VIOLET.
BUDDY KISSED ME
HE KISSED ME FOR THE FIRST TIME
DAISY.
DIDN'T YOU HEAR WHAT HE SAID?
VIOLET.
THERE'S ONLY ONE THOUGHT
RUNNING THROUGH MY HEAD
HE KISSED ME
DAISY.
AND THEN THEY BOTH DENIED
ANY THOUGHT OF ROMANCE
VIOLET.
BUT HE KISSED ME
WORDS CAN LIE
BUT KISSES DON'T
DAISY.
YOU CAN LIE TO YOURSELF
I WON'T
NO ONE COULD LOVE A SIAMESE TWIN
NOBODY WANTS US

DAISY. (Cont.)
NO ONE EVER HAS
NO ONE EVER WILL
  VIOLET.
WHY ARE YOU TRYING TO KILL MY DREAM?
  DAISY.
IT'S NOT A DREAM
IT'S A NIGHTMARE
WAKE UP
LOOK AROUND YOU
WE ARE FREAKS
STUCK TOGETHER
AND WE'LL ALWAYS BE ALONE
  VIOLET.
BUT I WANT TO WAKE UP
TO WHAT I'M DREAMING OF
DREAMING THAT SOME DAY
SOME NIGHT
I COULD FIND LOVE
WILL I FIND LOVE?

LIKE A FISH PLUCKED FROM THE OCEAN
TOSSED INTO A FOREIGN STREAM
ALWAYS KNEW THAT I WAS DIFFERENT
OFTEN FLED INTO A DREAM
I IGNORED THE RAGING CURRENTS
RIGHT AGAINST THE TIDE I SWAM
BUT I FLOATED WITH THE QUESTION
WHO WILL LOVE ME AS I AM?
  DAISY.
LIKE AN ODD EXOTIC CREATURE
ON DISPLAY INSIDE A ZOO
HEARING CHILDREN ASKING QUESTIONS
MAKES ME ASK SOME QUESTIONS TOO
COULD WE BEND THE LAWS OF NATURE?
COULD A LION LOVE A LAMB?
WHO COULD SEE BEYOND THIS SURFACE?
WHO WILL LOVE ME AS I AM?
  DAISY and VIOLET.
WHO WILL EVER CALL TO SAY I LOVE YOU?
SEND ME FLOWERS OR A TELEGRAM?
WHO COULD PROUDLY STAND BESIDE ME?
WHO WILL LOVE ME AS I AM?

DAISY.
LIKE A CLOWN WHOSE TEARS CAUSE LAUGHTER
TRAPPED INSIDE THE CENTER RING
   VIOLET.
EVEN SEEING SMILING FACES
I AM LONELY PONDERING
   DAISY and VIOLET.
WHO WOULD WANT TO JOIN THIS MADNESS?
WHO WOULD CHANGE MY MONOGRAM?
WHO WILL BE PART OF MY CIRCUS?
WHO WILL LOVE ME AS I AM?

WHO WILL EVER CALL TO SAY I LOVE YOU?
SEND ME FLOWERS OR A TELEGRAM?
WHO COULD PROUDLY STAND BESIDE ME?
WHO WILL LOVE ME AS I AM?
   COMPANY. *(Entering.)*
WHO COULD PROUDLY STAND BESIDE ME
WHO WILL LOVE ME AS I AM?

END OF ACT I

ACT II

Scene 1 - THE FOLLIES

(DAISY and VIOLET appear as lovebirds with the COMPANY, also costumed as birds, in an elaborate Ziegfeld-type number evoking the HILTON SISTERS at the height of their fame.)

(#16 "Rare Songbirds on Display")

DAISY and VIOLET.
WE'RE SINGING SWEET BIRD SONGS OF LO-VE
AS WE FLOAT AND FLUTTER ABO-VE
AND EACH LITTLE SPARROW AND DOVE WANTS TO PLAY
OUR LOVE SONGS ARE MUSIC FOR MATING
BUT THESE LITTLE LOVEBIRDS ARE WAITING
WILL SOMEONE FIND US CAPTIVATING PREY?
WE'LL KEEP SINGING ...
   ALL. (DAISY and VIOLET.)
... TILL THAT DAY
THEY'RE (WE'RE) SONGBIRDS ON DISPLAY
   ALL.
TWO BIRDS IN FLIGHT
DELIGHTING FAR ABOVE THE FRAY
THEY'RE WINGING
THEY'RE SINGING
THEY'RE BRINGING MELODIES OUR WAY
AH—WHAT A FEATHER SPRAY
RARE SONGBIRDS ON DISPLAY
AH AH

69

Scene 2 - BACKSTAGE

(As the set for the preceding number breaks down around them, BUDDY, wearing white tie and tails, joins DAISY and VIOLET.)

(#16A "Good Show, You Two")

BUDDY.
GOOD SHOW, YOU TWO
VIOLET.
REMEMBER WHEN THE COMPLIMENTS
CAME WITH KISSES?
DAISY.
NOT ANY MORE
PEOPLE MIGHT TALK
VIOLET.
IMAGINE WHAT THEY'D SAY
BUDDY.
THAT'S NOT FAIR
THE TABLOIDS KEEP TRYING
TO LINK YOU TO US
WHY ADD FUEL TO THE FIRE?
DAISY.
WHY NOT?
THEY WRITE WHATEVER THEY WANT
VIOLET.
GOD FORBID THEY SHOULD MENTION YOU
IN CONNECTION WITH US
BUDDY.
VIOLET, NOTHING MAKES ME PROUDER
THAN WORKING WITH YOU
AND YOU KNOW IT
VIOLET.
SOMETIMES I DO

(JAKE enters, also dressed in white tie and tails.)

JAKE.
LET'S GET CRACKIN', YOU TWO
WE CAN'T BE LATE FOR THE PARTY

BUDDY.
WHAT AN EXCITING NIGHT
NEW YORK SOCIETY COMING TO MEET YOU
   DAISY.
I CAN'T WAIT
   VIOLET.
I CAN
   DAISY.
BEING THE TOAST OF THE TOWN
IS SUCH A HARDSHIP FOR HER
   VIOLET.
PEOPLE POINT AND STARE
   BUDDY.
BUT THIS CROWD DOES IT WITH FLAIR
   DAISY.
AND WE HAVE BEAUTIFUL GOWNS TO WEAR
   JAKE.
WAIT TILL YOU SEE THEM
TAKE IT FROM A CANNIBAL
GOOD ENOUGH TO EAT
   VIOLET.
YOU'RE VERY SWEET
BUT STOP FUSSING OVER ME
   DAISY.
WE WANT YOU TO HAVE FUN
   BUDDY.
I'LL SEE TO THAT
   JAKE.
SO WILL I
   VIOLET.
ALL RIGHT
I'LL TRY
   BUDDY. That's all we ask. Now you two go get changed.

(DAISY and VIOLET exit.)

(#17 "Does Violet Seem Unhappy to You?")

   BUDDY. (Cont.)
DOES VIOLET SEEM UNHAPPY TO YOU?
   JAKE.
MAYBE SO

BUDDY.
DO YOU KNOW WHY?
JAKE.
MAYBE SO
BUDDY.
YOU KNOW I'D DO ANYTHING TO HELP HER
JAKE.
ONLY GUESSING
BUT REMEMBER WHEN
YOU FIRST MET THE GIRLS
AND THEY TOLD YOU THEIR DREAMS
BUDDY.
LIKE IT WAS YESTERDAY
JAKE.
WELL DAISY'S DREAM HAS COME TRUE
THEY'RE FAMOUS NOW
BUDDY.
BUT VIOLET DOESN'T HAVE A HUSBAND
JAKE.
SHE COULD
BUDDY.
OF COURSE
SHE'S A WONDERFUL WOMAN
BUT SHE IS A SIAMESE TWIN
JAKE.
THAT WOULDN'T MATTER TO ME
BUDDY.
TO YOU?
JAKE.
I MEAN IT WOULDN'T MATTER
TO SOMEONE WHO LOVES HER
TERRY. *(Entering, also in white tie and tails.)* Well, gentlemen.
If you had any doubts, this evening is proof we have arrived.
BUDDY. We dressed for the occasion
JAKE. Not bad for some bums from the sideshow.
BUDDY. Speak for yourself.
TERRY. I'm so confident about our future, I've resigned from
the Orpheum Circuit.
BUDDY. You're kidding.
TERRY. I can't stand to be away from our girls.
WE'VE GOT ROSY RED DAYS AHEAD
UNDER DREAMY BLUE CLOUDLESS SKY

BUDDY.
WE WERE MAKING DO
JAKE.
NOW WE'RE MAKING HAY
TERRY.
LET'S MAKE THE MOST OF
TERRY, BUDDY, JAKE.
THIS NEW YEAR'S DAY
BUDDY.
EVERYTHING'S NEW
JAKE.
NEW LIFE
TERRY.
NEW YORK
TERRY, BUDDY, JAKE.
NEW YEAR'S EVE!

(The THREE turn Upstage as the ROUSTABOUTS, wearing tuxedos, help change the set.)

Scene 3 - NEW YEAR'S EVE PARTY

(A fashionable party is revealed, filled with snobbish GUESTS.)

(#18 "New Year's Eve")

TERRY.
THANKS FOR ATTENDING OUR PARTY
WE'LL CHEER AS THE NEW YEAR BEGINS
LET'S HEAR ONE NOW
MAKE IT HEARTY
HERE THEY ARE
THE HILTON TWINS!

(DAISY and VIOLET enter dressed in beautiful gowns)

DAISY and VIOLET.
WE HAVE HAD AN AMAZING YEAR
WE'RE SO GLAD OUR NEW FRIENDS ARE HERE

DAISY.
YOU COULD BE IN ROME
VIOLET.
MADRID OR ST. TROPEZ
DAISY and VIOLET.
WE'RE PLEASED YOU JOINED US
FOR NEW YEAR'S DAY
GUEST 1.
WHICH SIAMESE TWIN IS WHICH?
DAISY.
I'M DAISY
VIOLET.
I'M VIOLET
DAISY and VIOLET.
WE'RE NOT SIAMESE
GUEST 2.
THEN WHAT ARE YOU?
DAISY and VIOLET.
TWINS
WHO ARE CONJOINED
GUEST 3.
WHATEVER YOU ARE
DON'T YOU WANT TO BE NORMAL?
VIOLET.
WHOEVER YOU ARE
DON'T YOU?
GUEST 4.
DON'T YOU WANT HUSBANDS?
DAISY.
IS THAT A PROPOSAL?
GUEST 5.
WHAT IF IT IS?
DAISY.
SORRY
I'M ALREADY ATTACHED
GUEST 6.
COULD YOU HAVE CHILDREN?
VIOLET.
NOT WITH YOU
GUEST 7.
BUT COULD YOU?
WITH YOUR CONDITION?

VIOLET.
THE SO-CALLED SIAMESE TWINS
CHANG AND ENG
HAD WIVES
AND TWENTY-TWO KIDS
   DAISY.
BUT RIGHT NOW WE'RE MUCH TOO BUSY
WITH OUR CAREER
   VIOLET.
AS WE CELEBRATE
A BRAND NEW YEAR
   DAISY.
THE PARTY'S JUST BEGUN
   VIOLET.
ENJOY YOURSELVES
   DAISY and VIOLET.
HAVE FUN

(#18 "Tango & Proposal")

(Tango music begins. As the PARTY GUESTS dance, BUDDY does some mock tango moves with DAISY and VIOLET to try to get VIOLET to laugh. DAISY turns Upstage where she converses with TERRY as BUDDY talks with VIOLET.)

   BUDDY.
VIOLET, WHAT'S WRONG?
I CAN TELL YOU'RE NOT HAPPY
   VIOLET.
IT'S NEW YEAR'S EVE
DOESN'T EVERYONE GET BLUE?
   BUDDY.
NOT ME
I'M WITH MY FAVORITE GIRL
   VIOLET.
YOU MEAN "BUSINESS ASSOCIATE"
   BUDDY.
VIOLET
   VIOLET.
THAT'S WHAT YOU TELL REPORTERS
   BUDDY.
THOSE IDIOTS
THEY DON'T DESERVE THE TRUTH

VIOLET.
WHAT IS THE TRUTH?
BUDDY.
OUR FRIENDSHIP GOES DEEPER
THAN WORKING TOGETHER
VIOLET.
DEEPER?
BUDDY.
A BOTTOMLESS WELL OF LOVE
VIOLET.
LOVE?
BUDDY.
WHAT ELSE COULD IT BE?
HAVE YOU EVER FELT THIS WAY
WITH ANYONE BEFORE?
VIOLET.
I HAVEN'T
HAVE YOU?
BUDDY.
YOU'RE THE FAM'LY I NEVER HAD
THE FRIEND I'VE ALWAYS WANTED
VIOLET.
I'M GLAD
    BUDDY. Good. Could I see a smile please?
    VIOLET. I guess so.
    BUDDY.
WHAT DO I HAVE TO DO?
GET DOWN ON MY KNEES FOR YOU?
I'M GETTING DOWN ON MY KNEES
BEGGING YOU TO SMILE ...
    VIOLET. You're embarrassing me.
    BUDDY. And making you laugh a little?
    TERRY. Hey, Buddy, what's going on over there? You look like you're proposing.
    VIOLET. He's making fun of me.
    BUDDY. I am not. Violet refuses to believe I love her.
    DAISY. You do?
    BUDDY. Of course.
    TERRY. Then you are proposing.
    VIOLET. He's not.
    BUDDY. Would that make you happy?
    DAISY. Couldn't hurt.
    VIOLET. Daisy.

TERRY. What a story that would make.

DAISY. Can I be the maid of honor?

VIOLET. Stop it! All of you. Stop making fun of me.

BUDDY. Oh, Violet. No. Please don't cry. That's the last thing I want.

VIOLET. I'm sorry. I can't joke about this.

BUDDY. This isn't a joke.

(#18B "New Year's Eve")

VIOLET, I LOVE YOU
I DON'T KNOW HOW ELSE TO SAY IT
I WANT YOU TO BE MY WIFE
I DREAM OF YOU SHARING MY LIFE

Violet Hilton, you make me so happy. Allow me to do the same. Marry me.

DAISY. *(After a pause, whispering to VIOLET.)* If you don't say yes I'm going to have a heart attack that will kill us both.

BUDDY.
WHAT ARE YOU WAITING FOR
WHAT'S SO HARD?

VIOLET.
I'M CAUGHT BY SURPRISE
CAUGHT OFF-GUARD
NEVER TRUSTED GOOD TIMES
OR SUCCESS
NOW I'M TRUSTING MY HEART
I'M SAYING YES, BUDDY
I'LL MARRY YOU

BUDDY.	
WE'VE GOT HEAVENLY	
NIGHTS TO SHARE	**VIOLET.**
	HEAVENLY NIGHTS TO
	SHARE
WE'VE GOT SHOOTING	
STARS TO OUTSHINE	
	SHOOTING STARS

BUDDY and VIOLET.
AND OUR SHOT AT THE MOON
CAN'T MISS OR RICOCHET

TERRY.
LET'S MAKE IT PUBLIC
FOR NEW YEAR'S DAY

BUDDY.
WHAT ABOUT A BIG DOUBLE WEDDING?
VIOLET.
OH WHAT A SPLENDID DISPLAY
DAISY.
COULD IT BE THAT'S WHERE WE'RE HEADING?
TERRY.
TIME TO WELCOME
NEW YEAR'S DAY
VIOLET, BUDDY, TERRY and DAISY.
WE'VE GOT ROSY RED DAYS AHEAD
UNDER DREAMY BLUE CLOUDLESS SKY
WE'VE GOT YEARS OF BLISS
TO KISS AWAY EACH DAY
HERE'S TO THE GOOD TIMES
WE'RE ON OUR WAY
TERRY.
LOVE IS THE LEAD IN
FOR NEW YEAR'S DAY

(The ROUSTABOUTS start striking the party set, leaving a bare stage. TERRY makes an announcement to the GUESTS.)

TERRY. (Cont.) Ladies and gents, the hour is upon us. And I've got big news with which to welcome the year. The lovely Violet Hilton has accepted a marriage proposal from Mr. Buddy Foster!
ALL.
WE'VE GOT ROSY RED DAYS AHEAD
UNDER DREAMY BLUE CLOUDLESS SKY
AS THE OLD YEAR WANES
LOVE WILL LEAD THE WAY
HERE'S TO A NEW LOVE
MAY IT BE TRUE LOVE
ONE-MADE-FROM-TWO LOVE
FOR NEW YEAR'S DAY
FOR NEW YEAR'S DAY
FOR NEW YEAR'S DAY

(In slow motion, the GUESTS exchange embraces and New Year's Eve kisses.)

DAISY. *(To VIOLET.)* Happy New Year.
VIOLET. *(To DAISY.)* Happy New Year.

(BUDDY kisses VIOLET. TERRY moves into kiss DAISY, but stops and turns away.)

(#18C "Auld Lang Syne")

PARTY GUEST.
SHOULD OLD ACQUAINTANCE
  ADD 2 PARTY GUESTS.
BE FORGOT AND NEVER BROUGHT TO MIND
  VIOLET. Jake, I'm finally getting married!
  3 PARTY GUESTS.
SHOULD OLD ACQUAINTANCE BE FORGOT
  JAKE. Buddy's a lucky guy.
  TERRY. Our guests are leaving. You girls go make your good-byes.

(DAISY and VIOLET exit after GUESTS. JAKE follows, leaving BUDDY and TERRY alone.)

GUESTS.
AND THE DAYS OF AULD LANG SYNE
  TERRY. Brilliant move, Buddy.
  BUDDY. What do you mean?
  TERRY. Asking Violet to marry you. It's the story of the year—the decade!
  BUDDY. That's not why I did it.
  TERRY. Of course not.
  BUDDY. I can't stand to see her unhappy and now she won't be.
  TERRY. Everyone benefits.
  BUDDY. Hey, why don't you marry Daisy? Since there's such an obvious connection between you two.
  TERRY. Obvious connection? Maybe to her way of thinking.
  BUDDY. Only hers?
  TERRY. You go ahead. I need to get some air.

(BUDDY exits.)

Scene 4 - BARE STAGE

(#19 "Private Conversation")

TERRY.
AN OBVIOUS CONNECTION
I TRIED SO HARD TO HIDE
COULDN'T EVEN SAY IT TO MYSELF
AN OBVIOUS CONNECTION
I TRIED TO PUSH ASIDE
INTO A CORNER
ON THE DARKEST SHELF

WE'LL NEVER BE ALONE
AND MY FEELINGS CAN'T BE SHOWN
SO I TRY TO IMAGINE AND REPLAY
ALL THE THINGS I'LL NEVER GET TO SAY
YOU'RE WRAPPED UP WITH ANOTHER
TANGLED AND ENTWINED
I INVENT A SEPARATION
IN THE PRIVATE CONVERSATION
IN MY MIND

I RESOLVE TO SAY IT ALL
THEN I HEM AND HAW AND STALL
FOR HOW COULD I COME CLEAN
OR CONFIDE
SOMEONE ELSE IS ALWAYS AT YOUR SIDE

I WANT
I WANT
I WANT TO TELL YOU
I WANT
I WANT
TO GET YOU ALONE
I NEED
I NEED
I NEED TO TELL YOU
I WANT YOU FOR MY OWN
IF WE COULD STEAL A MOMENT

TERRY. (Cont.)
WOULD YOU BE SO INCLINED
TO ACCEPT AN INVITATION
TO THE PRIVATE CONVERSATION
IN MY MIND

(DAISY appears alone, Upstage.)

DAISY.
WHAT DO YOU WANT
TO SAY TO ME, TERRY?
TELL ME, THIS IS YOUR CHANCE
WHAT DO YOU NEED
TO SAY TO ME, TERRY
DOES IT CONCERN ROMANCE?

HERE I AM
ALL ALONE
YOURS TO TAKE
SMOOTH ME OUT
CALM ME DOWN
STOP THE ACHE

DON'T HOLD BACK
DON'T HOLD OFF
HOLD ME TIGHT
DON'T OBJECT
LET'S CONNECT
LET'S UNITE
TERRY.
BUT YOU CAN'T LOSE YOUR SHADOW
THAT TIE YOU CAN'T UNBIND
DAISY.
YOU'VE MADE US ALL ALONE NOW
TERRY.
ALL ALONE
BUT ONLY IN MY MIND
DAISY.
A MIND IS VERY PRIVATE
WE OFTEN MEET IN MINE
LET ME SHOW YOU WHAT WE DO THERE
THE WAY WE KISS
THE WAY WE INTERTWINE

DAISY. (Cont.)
I WANT
I WANT
I WANT TO SHOW YOU
    TERRY.
SHOW ME WHAT?
    DAISY.
I WANT TO SHOW YOU DESIRE
THE HEAT
THE FLAMES
    TERRY.
I'M BURNING FOR YOU
    DAISY.
I KNOW YOU ARE ON FIRE

WHY NOT BE BOLD
I'M CRAZY ABOUT YOU
I SAY IT WITH EVERY GLANCE
MY ARMS ARE COLD
AND LAZY WITHOUT YOU
COME ON
WHY DON'T WE DANCE

(Tentatively DAISY turns TERRY toward her, puts his hand on her hip and they begin to dance, slowly at first, then swirling around the stage. Finally, they kiss.)

    TERRY.
I WANT
I WANT
I WANT TO KEEP YOU
    DAISY.
KEEP ME WHERE?

(VIOLET appears Upstage.)

    TERRY.
I WANT YOU ALL FOR MY OWN
MY OWN
MY OWN
    DAISY. *(Breaking away from him.)*
YOU HAVE TO SHARE ME

TERRY.
OH NO
I WANT YOU ALONE

(But DAISY joins VIOLET and they disappear.)

TERRY. (Cont.)
I IMAGINE US SO WELL
HOW YOU'D DANCE AND TASTE AND SMELL
I CAN IMAGINE
ME WITH YOU
BUT I DON'T HAVE THE GUT
TO FOLLOW THROUGH
YOU'RE ONE HALF OF A COUPLE
THAT'S HOW YOU ARE DEFINED
AND MY ONLY CONSOLATION
IS THE PRIVATE CONVERSATION
IN MY MIND

(TERRY turns and slowly crosses Upstage to where DAISY joined VIOLET. BUDDY appears as the music suddenly turns jaunty.)

Scene 5 - ON THE ROAD

(BUDDY, dressed for performance, sings and dances in a spotlight.)

*(#20 "**One Plus One Equals Three**")*

BUDDY.
I NEVER SOUGHT THE SPOTLIGHT
I STAYED BEHIND THE SCENES
BUT THEN I MET A SWEETHEART
WHO CHANGED MY OLD ROUTINES
SHE PUT ME IN THE SPOTLIGHT
NOW I'M A HAPPY PUP
AND WHEN I COUNT MY BLESSINGS
I FIND THEY ALL ADD UP
TO

BUDDY. (Cont.)
ONE PLUS ONE EQUALS THREE
MY BABY, HER SISTER AND ME
THIS IS NOT WHAT I EXPECTED
BUT MY BABY IS WELL-CONNECTED
YOU CAN SEE WHY I ELECTED
THIS ARITHMETIC WITH AN ODD KEY
WHERE ONE PLUS ONE EQUALS THREE

SOME GUYS
WONDER HOW IT WILL WORK
SOME WOMEN
TITTER AND SMIRK
ALL THEIR QUESTIONS WILL BE RESOLVED
I'VE GOT THE PROBLEM SOLVED
'CAUSE ONE PLUS ONE
ONE PLUS ONE
ONE PLUS ONE

(DAISY and VIOLET enter.)

(#20A "One Plus One Equals Three" Pt. 2)

DAISY and VIOLET. We've always been a duo
DAISY. A twosome who's compact
DAISY and VIOLET. But we're happy to welcome
VIOLET. An addition to our act
DAISY. He's Violet's intended
BUDDY. I'm the lucky one
VIOLET. I'm the one who's lucky
DAISY, VIOLET, BUDDY. Ain't we having fun!
BUDDY.
WE'RE PLANNING A BIG WEDDING
FOR EACH AND EV'RY FRIEND
CONSIDER THIS YOUR INVITATION
DAISY and VIOLET. Hope you will attend!
BUDDY, DAISY, VIOLET.
BIG DAY
WILL BE COMING UP SOON
BIG WEDDING
BUDDY and VIOLET.
SMALL HONEYMOON

BUDDY, VIOLET, DAISY.
FOR THE MOMENT WE THOUGHT WE'D DO
THIS PREVIEW JUST FOR YOU

(Set changes to radio station. BUDDY, DAISY and VIOLET step up to microphones and are joined by the three VALE SISTERS at another mike.)

VALE SISTERS.
OOO-OOO-OOO
OOO-OOO-OOO
OOO-OOO-OOO
DAISY, VIOLET, VALE SISTERS.
HEY THERE, PROFESSOR
WON'TCHA ANSWER, YES SIR!
HOW-ZABOUT A LESSON
IN YOUR NEW KIND A MATH?

(#20B "One Plus One Equals Three" Pt. 3)

BUDDY.
WELL ...
ONE PLUS ONE EQUALS ... ?
DAISY, VIOLET, VALE SISTERS.
THAT'S GONNA BE
GONNA BE THREE
VIOLET.
HIS BABY
DAISY.
HER SISTER
BUDDY.
AND DON'T FORGET ME
VALE SISTERS.
IT'S NOT YOUR AVERAGE EQUATION
NOT YOUR STANDARD OCCASION
BUDDY.
WITH A LITTLE PERSUASION
HOW HAP-HAP-HAP-HAP-HAPPY WE'LL BE
WHEN ONE PLUS ONE
DAISY, VIOLET, VALE SISTERS.
PLUS ONE
BUDDY.
ONE PLUS ONE

DAISY, VIOLET, VALE SISTERS.
WHAT FUN!
   BUDDY.
ONE PLUS ONE
MEANS MY BABY

DAISY.	**VALE SISTERS.**
I'M HIS BABY	... HIS BABY

   BUDDY.
HER SISTER

DAISY.	**VALE SISTERS.**
I'M HIS BABY'S SISTER	... HIS BABY'S SISTER
AND ...	AND ...

   BUDDY.
AND ME
   VALE SISTERS.
THAT EQUALS
   VIOLET.
AND ME
   VALE SISTERS.
THAT EQUALS
   DAISY.
AND ME
   VALE SISTERS.
THAT EQUALS
   BUDDY, DAISY, VIOLET, VALE SISTERS.
EQUALS THREE!

*(On applause, VALE SISTERS exit. JAKE enters and helps DAISY
   and VIOLET remove their wraps and sit on stools.)*

(#24 "Buddy, You're a Wonderful Performer")

   VIOLET.
BUDDY, YOU'RE A WONDERFUL PERFORMER
YOU'VE BECOME THE STAR I KNEW YOU'D BE
   BUDDY.
YOU GIVE ME CONFIDENCE OUT THERE
   VIOLET.
YOU GET SO NERVOUS
BEFORE THE SHOW
YOU REMIND ME OF ME

TERRY. *(Entering.)* Good work, everyone. I'm expecting a call up in the office. Then I'm taking us to dinner.
BUDDY. I'll come with you.

(BUDDY kisses VIOLET and follows TERRY Off.)

VIOLET. *(Taking note of DAISY's glum expression.)* You know, Daisy, before long you'll be getting married and I'll be the brides-maid.
DAISY. Don't hold your breath. I'm not feeling well. I want to go home.
VIOLET. Anything I can do?
DAISY. I don't think so.
VIOLET. Jake, could you tell Buddy and Terry to go ahead with-out us. We'll wait here for you.
JAKE. I'll tell 'em.

(JAKE exits.)

Scene 6A - RADIO STATION OFFICE

(BUDDY and TERRY appear above DAISY and VIOLET.)

(#21A "I Need To Talk to You")

BUDDY.
I NEED TO TALK TO YOU
    TERRY.
IS SOMETHING WRONG?
    BUDDY.
I'M WORRIED ABOUT DAISY
THE QUESTIONS PEOPLE ASK
SHE'S BOUND TO FEEL LEFT OUT
    TERRY.
SHE'S GETTING MORE ATTENTION THAN EVER
    BUDDY.
BUT VIOLET IS THE FOCUS

TERRY.
THEY'RE USED TO SHARING
   BUDDY.
THEN HOW ABOUT THAT DOUBLE WEDDING?
   TERRY.
WOULD YOU STOP WITH THAT
I COULD NEVER MARRY A SIAMESE TWIN
   BUDDY.
I DON'T SEE HER AS A SIAMESE TWIN
I GOT OVER THAT LONG AGO
   TERRY.
YOU'RE A BETTER MAN THAN I
   BUDDY.
AND NOW I'M MAKING HER DREAM COME TRUE
AND THAT MAKES ME HAPPY
   TERRY.
NOT TO MENTION FAMOUS
   BUDDY.
AN UNEXPECTED BENEFIT
WHICH I ADMIT I REALLY LIKE
   TERRY.
YOU KNOW SHE REALLY LOVES YOU
   BUDDY.
AND I LOVE HER
   TERRY.
IS IT LOVE
OR PITY

(JAKE enters the area unseen by TERRY and BUDDY.)

   TERRY. Whatever your reasons for proposing, there's a lot riding
on this wedding.
AND NOTHING'S GONNA STOP IT
NOT DAISY
NOT VIOLET
NOT YOU
   BUDDY.
THIS IS MY CHANCE
TO DO SOMETHING IMPORTANT
TO BE REMEMBERED
TO MAKE A BIG SPLASH
   TERRY.
THEN I'M DEPENDING ON YOU

TERRY. (Cont.)
TO KEEP THIS ON TRACK
KEEP PLAYING YOUR PART
KEEP VIOLET CONTENT
KEEP THE HAPPY COUPLE HAPPY

(JAKE leaves.)

    BUDDY.
THAT'S NOT A PROBLEM
BUT DAISY COULD BE
    TERRY.
I'LL TAKE CARE OF HER
    BUDDY.
ON THE HONEYMOON?

(TERRY exits.)

    BUDDY. (Cont.)
YOU ACT LIKE YOU KNOW
WHAT'S BEHIND EVERY DOOR
I ONLY HOPE
THAT I'M NOT GETTING MORE
THAN I BARGAINED FOR

(BUDDY exits as lights dim on that area.)

Scene 6B - DESERTED RADIO STATION

(Lights up on DAISY and VIOLET seated on stools as in the previous
    scene.)
(#21B "Oh Daisy, How Can I Make This Easier")

    VIOLET.
OH, DAISY
HOW CAN I MAKE THIS EASIER FOR YOU?
    DAISY.
YOU CAN'T
I CAN BARELY GET THROUGH THE SONGS
HOW WILL I GET THROUGH YOUR WEDDING
OR HONEYMOON?

VIOLET.
YOU WILL CLOSE A DOOR INSIDE
   DAISY.
I CAN'T
WHEN BUDDY HOLDS YOUR HAND
I TINGLE ALL OVER
WHEN HE PECKS YOU ON THE CHEEK
I FEEL IT ON MINE
   VIOLET.
WE'VE ALWAYS LEARNED TO ADJUST
WE CAN LEARN ...
   DAISY.
YOU'RE THE BRIDE
YOU'LL BE PREOCCUPIED

(JAKE enters their area.)

   VIOLET.
IF I WERE YOU ...
   DAISY.
YOU'RE NOT
   VIOLET.
YOU'RE JUST JEALOUS
   DAISY.
OF COURSE I AM
   JAKE.
THERE'S NOTHING TO BE JEALOUS ABOUT
   VIOLET.
WHAT DO YOU MEAN?
   JAKE.
DON'T GO THROUGH WITH THIS WEDDING
   VIOLET.
JAKE, WHAT'S GOTTEN INTO YOU?
   JAKE.
I FEEL THINGS
I KNOW THINGS
   VIOLET.
SO DO I
BUDDY WILL MAKE ME HAPPY
   JAKE.
I WANT YOUR HAPPINESS
MORE THAN ANYTHING
BUT I DON'T TRUST THIS ...

VIOLET.
AND WHAT DO YOU KNOW ABOUT IT?
JAKE.
I KNOW PLENTY
I KNOW HOW SOMEONE SHOULD LOVE YOU
VIOLET. And how is that?

(#22 "You Should Be Loved")

JAKE.
YOU SHOULD BE LOVED
BY SOMEONE WHO KNOWS YOU
WANTS YOU TO BLOSSOM
ALWAYS IS TRUE
YOU SHOULD BE CHERISHED
LIKE THE FIRST SIGN OF SPRINGTIME
YOU SHOULD BE LOVED ...

YOU SHOULD BE LOVED
WITH CONSTANT DEVOTION
HEART-POUNDING PASSION
FLOODING YOU THROUGH
YOU SHOULD BE TREASURED
LIKE A RUBY OR A DIAMOND
YOU SHOULD BE LOVED
IN THE WAY
I LOVE YOU

ALL THROUGH THE YEARS
I'VE HELD OCEANS INSIDE
HELD BACK THE TEARS
AND THE WAVES AND THE TIDE
THE DAM HAD TO BURST
AND THE CURRENTS COLLIDE
WITH THE FLOOD OF EMOTION
I CAN NO LONGER HIDE

WE SHOULD BE CLOSE
AS STARS ARE TO HEAVEN
SHORELINE TO OCEAN
BIRDS TO THE BLUE
WE SHOULD BE COUPLED
WITH A LIFETIME CONNECTION

JAKE. (Cont.)
WE SHOULD BE JOINED
LIKE WE'RE ONE
AND NOT TWO
YES YOU SHOULD BE LOVED
IN THE WAY
I LOVE YOU
    VIOLET.
JAKE
OF COURSE WE LOVE EACH OTHER
LIKE A BROTHER AND SISTER
OR MOTHER AND CHILD
NOT IN A WAY THAT IS WILD
LIKE ...
    JAKE.
HAVEN'T YOU HEARD WHAT I'M SAYING?
I AM IN LOVE WITH YOU
    VIOLET.
OH, JAKE
OH NO
I NEVER THOUGHT
NEVER FELT ...
    JAKE.
WHAT I FELT?
    VIOLET.
I NEVER KNEW
    JAKE.
WELL NOW YOU DO
    VIOLET.
YOU KNOW ME BETTER THAN ANYONE
EXCEPT DAISY
YOU'VE ALWAYS BEEN MORE THAN A FRIEND
YOU KNOW I DON'T LONG
TO SEE PARIS OR ROME
ALL THAT I WANT
IS A HUSBAND AND HOME
    JAKE.
I COULD BE BOTH
    VIOLET.
THE WORLD WON'T LET YOU
    JAKE.
I DON'T CARE ABOUT THEM
ONLY YOU
WITH LOVE

JAKE. (Cont.)
WE COULD RISE ABOVE
THE WHISPERS AND STARES
WE COULD CHALLENGE THE POWERS OF FATE
WE COULD MASTER A BAD CIRCUMSTANCE
IF YOU GIVE ME A CHANCE

JAKE.	**VIOLET.**
WE SHOULD BE CLOSE	WE ARE CLOSE
AS STARS ARE TO HEAVEN	LIKE A BROTHER AND
	SISTER
SHORELINE TO OCEAN	
BIRDS TO THE BLUE	MOTHER AND CHILD
WE SHOULD BE COUPLED	
WITH A LIFETIME	THE WORLD WON'T
CONNECTION	LET US
WE SHOULD BE JOINED	
LIKE WE'RE ONE	I KNOW WHAT
AND NOT TWO	PEOPLE DO
YES YOU SHOULD BE LOVED	I AM LOVED
IN THE WAY	AND IN MY WAY
I LOVE YOU	I LOVE YOU

VIOLET.
I WANT TO BE LIKE EVERYONE ELSE
I COULDN'T BEAR
WHAT THEY WOULD SAY
IF I LOVED YOU THAT WAY

(TERRY and BUDDY enter excitedly.)

TERRY. Great news—Texas has come through!

BUDDY. And not only with a marriage license.

TERRY. Tell her, Buddy.

BUDDY. Violet, our wedding is going to be the grand finale of the Texas Centennial! Can you believe it?

TERRY. Right there on the fifty-yard line of the Cotton Bowl—in front of thousands of people. You'll be on every front page in the country.

DAISY. Really.

TERRY. Let's go celebrate!

BUDDY. Jake, you come too. You're part of the family.

DAISY. That's right, Jake. You're family and always will be.

(TERRY, BUDDY, DAISY and VIOLET exit. The ROUSTABOUTS appear and stand threateningly around JAKE, then slowly move Upstage.)

(#22A "Cannibal King" [Reprise])

   JAKE.
IF I CAN SEE
PAST YOUR AFFLICTION
WHY CAN'T YOU SEE PAST MINE
WHY DO YOU CARE
WHAT PEOPLE MIGHT SAY
WHY TRY TO FIT INTO THEIR DESIGN
IF I HAD TOLD YOU
YOUR LOVE IS A LIE
WOULD YOU HAVE KISSED IT GOOD-BYE?

ONE OF THESE DAYS
YOU WILL LOOK BACK IN SHAME
AFTER YOU'VE LEARNED
THAT A SPARK'S NOT A FLAME
YOU WILL REGRET
HOW YOU PUSHED LOVE ASIDE
WHEN YOU'RE MARRIED TO NOTHING
WHEN YOU'RE MISERY'S BRIDE

YOU SHOULD BE LOVED
BY SOMEONE WHO WANTS YOU
TRIES TO PROTECT YOU
ALWAYS COMES THROUGH
YOU SHOULD HAVE CHOSEN
THE ONE WHO SUPPORTS YOU
ALWAYS SUPPORTS YOU
WHATEVER YOU DO
YES YOU SHOULD BE LOVED
IN THE WAY
I LOVE YOU

Scene 7 - THE TEXAS CENTENNIAL

(#22B " On Location")

(A Midway. DAISY, VIOLET, TERRY and BUDDY enter from Up-stage and cross through Carnival Pitchmen [the ROUSTABOUTS]

*urging them to try their games. The four cross Downstage Center
and look out as the Pitchmen exit.)*

(#23 *"Calliope on the Midway")*

TERRY. Just look at that!
VIOLET. It's the biggest billboard I've ever seen.
BUDDY. We're in Texas. Everything's the biggest.
DAISY. I don't see our names.
TERRY. Believe me—a mammoth sign that reads "Wedding of a
Siamese Twin"—people know it's referring to you.
DAISY. To me? I didn't know I was getting married.
BUDDY. Are you gonna start again?
DAISY. What if I am?
TERRY. Stay out of this, Buddy.
BUDDY. Are you gonna let her pout all through the wedding to-
morrow?
VIOLET. Buddy, Daisy is under a lot of strain.
BUDDY. Well so am I.
TERRY. Then be a man and deal with it.
BUDDY. All right. Jeez.
TERRY. Daisy, I know how difficult this is for you. But in the
bigger picture, it's helping you realize your dream.
DAISY. Is it?
TERRY. The whole country is talking about you.
DAISY. About me?
TERRY. It's understandable you feel neglected. I know I've been
too busy to give you the attention you deserve. We need some time
alone together, just the ... four of us.

(#24 *"Tunnel of Love")*

TERRY. (Cont.)
WE'RE ON A MIDWAY
A TEXAS-SIZED PLAYGROUND
LOTS OF DIVERSION AROUND
WE NEED DISTRACTION
WITHOUT TOO MUCH ACTION
LET ME SHOW YOU
A QUIET SPOT I'VE FOUND

Scene 8 - THE TUNNEL OF LOVE

(The Tunnel of Love ride appears Upstage and is slowly pushed Downstage by the ROUSTABOUTS until it is directly behind the Four.)

TERRY. (Cont.)
LET ME TAKE YOU TO
THE TUNNEL OF LOVE
DARK AND RELAXING INSIDE
ALL OF US COULD SHARE
THE TUNNEL OF LOVE
PLEASE COME ALONG FOR THE RIDE
WE NEED A BREAK
FROM THE PUSH AND THE SHOVE
WORK HAS US PREOCCUPIED
   TERRY and BUDDY.
WE CAN RELAX IN THE TUNNEL OF LOVE
   TERRY and BUDDY.
PLEASE COME ALONG

	VIOLET.	**DAISY.**
	I'LL COME ALONG	I'LL COME ALONG
FOR THE RIDE	FOR THE RIDE	FOR THE RIDE

(The Four get into the ride.)

   TERRY, DAISY, BUDDY, VIOLET, ROUSTABOUTS.
WE'RE GOING DOWN TO THE TUNNEL OF LOVE
WE'LL GET A BOAT AND EMBARK
WATER BELOW AND BLACKNESS ABOVE
   TERRY.
WE'LL BE ALONE, DAISY
      BUDDY.
      LIKE WE'RE ALONE, HONEY
         DAISY & VIOLET.
         ALMOST ALONE

IN THE DARK	IN THE DARK	IN THE DARK

(The ROUSTABOUTS lower a safety-bar and exit. The Four are spot-lighted individually during the following.)

DAISY.
DREAMED OF BEING CLOSE
NOW I'M PRESSING AGAINST HIS SIDE
DO I DARE TO MAKE AN ADVANCE?
HE'S NOT MADE A MOVE
SHOULD I SWALLOW MY GIRLISH PRIDE?
THIS COULD BE MY ONLY CHANCE
    BUDDY.
OUT THERE IN THE SPOTLIGHT
NEVER HAD A DOUBT I WANT YOU
WHY DO I FEEL PANIC
DOWN HERE IN THE DARK
VIOLET, I LOVE YOU
THOUGHT THAT LOVE WOULD LEAD TO PASSION
PASSION SHOULD BE PRIVATE
ME AND YOU
BUT I KNOW
SHE'S THERE TOO
    TERRY.
I HAD PLANNED TO KEEP THE TEMPERATURE COOL
SHE'S RAISING MY FAHRENHEIT
DON'T LET PASSION RULE YOU
DON'T BE A FOOL
DON'T FEED THAT APPETITE
OH WHAT THE HELL—WHY FIGHT?
    VIOLET.
WHAT IS GOING ON?
WHY DON'T BUDDY'S KISSES FEEL DIVINE
WHY DO DAISY'S SHIVERS RUN
UP MY SPINE
MUCH MORE PASSION FROM HER SIDE THAN MINE
BUDDY'S TAME
DAISY'S AFLAME
    VIOLET, BUDDY, DAISY, TERRY, ENSEMBLE.
SECRETS OF THE DARK
SECRETS OF LOVE
LONGING TO BE SATISFIED
THOUGH NO ON CAN SEE
IN THE TUNNEL OF LOVE

VIOLET, BUDDY, DAISY, TERRY, ENSEMBLE. (Cont.)
THERE'S NOT A PLACE I CAN HIDE.
　DAISY.
TERRY IS ON FIRE
ALL THE HEAT I'VE BEEN PRAYING FOR
　BUDDY.
I CAN'T EVEN TRY TO PRETEND
　VIOLET.
HE HAS NO DESIRE
　TERRY.
THESE ARE SINS I'LL BE PAYING FOR
　DAISY.
I HOPE THIS NEVER WILL END
　DAISY.
LOST IN THE DARKNESS
THE BOAT THAT I'M FLOATING IN
FEELS LIKE IT'S FLYING THROUGH SPACE
　　　　　　　　　　　　VIOLET.
　　　　　　I WANT TO LOSE MYSELF
　　　　　　ALL THE THOUGHTS OF WHO I AM
　　　　　　HERE IN HIS PRIVATE EMBRACE
　DAISY.
I THINK I MIGHT SINK
EDGING CLOSE TO THE BRINK
OF A DANGEROUS STEEP WATERFALL
OR AM I NOT MOVING AT ALL?
　　　　　　　　　　　　VIOLET.
　　　　　　ALL ALONE NOW
　　　　　　NO ONE IS WATCHING US
　　　　　　WHY NOT CLIMB OVER THE WALL?
　　　　　　TAKE ME A GIVE ME YOUR ALL
　DAISY.
GROPING MY WAY
TOWARD AN UNSTATED GOAL
DON'T KNOW WHERE I'M GOING
BUT FEEL LIKE I'VE BEEN THERE BEFORE
　　　　　　　　　　　　VIOLET.
　　　　　　SHOULDN'T YOU TAKE THE LEAD?
　　　　　　SHOULDN'T I FOLLOW?
　　　　　　SHOULDN'T YOU FILL THE NEED?
　　　　　　MY HEART IS HOLLOW
　DAISY.
I KNOW YOU ARE READY

DAISY. (Cont.)
I'M ON THE RIGHT TRACK
NO STOPPING NOW
NO TURNING BACK

        VIOLET.
        I WANT WHAT SHE'S GOT
        WHAT I'M FEELING SHE'S GOT
        EVERYTHING HE'S NOT YET
        FEELING WITH ME

DAISY.
I AM YOURS
YOU ARE MINE
IT'S A SIN
IT'S DIVINE   **VIOLET.**
        I WANT MINE
SO DIVINE

        WHERE IS MINE

(As TERRY ravages DAISY, VIOLET and BUDDY stare glumly ahead
   while the ride comes to a stop.)

ENSEMBLE.
SECRETS OF THE DARK
SECRETS OF LOVE
LONGING TO BE SATISFIED
THOUGH NO ONE CAN SEE
IN THE TUNNEL OF LOVE
THERE'S NOT A PLACE YOU CAN HIDE

(The ROUSTABOUTS raise the safety bar and DAISY, VIOLET,
   TERRY and BUDDY get out of the ride. The Two Couples blink
   and shield their eyes from the bright sunlight, each lost in thought.)

TERRY.
WAS THIS A MISTAKE
THE TUNNEL OF LOVE?
PASSION COULD NOT BE CONTROLLED
   BUDDY.
HOW CAN WE FORGET
THE TUNNEL OF LOVE?
   VIOLET.
WHY WAS I LEFT FEELING COLD?

    DAISY. (Cont.)
IN THE TUNNEL OF LOVE
WILL IT CONTINUE OUTSIDE?
    DAISY, VIOLET, TERRY, BUDDY, ENSEMBLE.
NOW THAT WE'RE OUT OF THE TUNNEL OF LOVE
GOTTA GET OFF
GOTTA GET OFF
GOTTA GET OFF
THIS RIDE
THIS RIDE
THIS RIDE

(As exit music plays, BUDDY storms off. VIOLET starts after him, as DAISY looks back over her shoulder at TERRY. He looks around quickly to see if anyone has observed this, then follows the others Offstage.)

(#24A "Scene Change")

Scene 9 - THE TEXAS CENTENNIAL

(The BOSS appears far Upstage.)

(#25 "Celebrate Love")

    THE BOSS.
LOVE
WE LOVE STORIES OF LOVE AND ROMANCE
LOVE CREATED IN SONG AND IN DANCE
ANY REMINDER THERE'S ALWAYS A CHANCE
LOVE COULD TRANSFORM OUR LIVES
LOVE
LOVE!

TICKETS, TICKETS
RIGHT THIS WAY
WEDDING SHOW TODAY

(The ROUSTABOUTS, dressed as HAWKERS, enter and join his spiel.)

THE BOSS and ROUSTABOUTS.
WEDDING
WEDDING
RIGHT THIS WAY
SEE THE SHOW TODAY

SEE THE GROOM
SEE THE BRIDE
SEE HER SISTER
BY HER SIDE

SEE THEM WED
AFTER NOON
SEE WHO'LL SHARE
THEIR HONEYMOON

(Four more HAWKERS enter.)

ADD FOUR MORE HAWKERS.
HERE
RIGHT HERE
GET A WEDDING SOUVENIR
REMEMBER THIS DAY
REMEMBER THIS FREAK SHOW
WITH A WEDDING MEMENTO

IN HONOR OF THE TWINS
DOUBLE HOT DOGS JOINED IN THE BUN
GET 'EM HOT
TWO FOR ONE
   HAWKER.
I GOT THE BEST
YOU ONLY HAVE TO ASK
GET A TWO-HEADED TWIN MASK
   THE BOSS and HAWKERS.
WHAT A BEAUTIFUL DAY FOR A WEDDING
WHAT AN EVENT TO VIEW
WHAT A STORY TO TELL YOUR CHILDREN
'CAUSE NEXT TO THE DAY
YOU BECAME MAN AND WIFE

THE BOSS and HAWKERS. (Cont.)
YOU'LL REMEMBER THIS WEDDING
FOR THE REST OF YOUR LIFE

LOVE ...
WE LOVE STORIES OF LOVE AND ROMANCE
LOVE CREATED IN SONG AND IN DANCE
ANY REMINDER THERE'S ALWAYS A CHANCE
LOVE COULD TRANSFORM OUR LIVES
LOVE
LOVE!

(During the previous stanza, DAISY and VIOLET enter, wearing matching dresses. ROUSTABOUTS change set to create area beneath the bleachers of the Cotton Bowl. The BOSS and HAWKERS exit as JAKE enters.)

Scene 10 - STADIUM DRESSING AREA

(#26 "Violet, I Always Knew You'd Make a Beautiful Bride")

JAKE.
VIOLET, I ALWAYS KNEW
YOU'D MAKE A BEAUTIFUL BRIDE
VIOLET.
THANK YOU, JAKE
YOU'RE VERY KIND
JAKE.
I'VE MADE UP MY MIND
I'M LEAVING
VIOLET.
FOR WHERE?
JAKE.
A FRIEND HAS A PLACE IN CHICAGO
SERVING BLUES LATE INTO THE NIGHT
WANTS ME TO HELP WITH PERFORMERS
THANKS TO YOU
I THINK I'LL DO ALRIGHT
WHY NOT GO?
DAISY.
BUT WE NEED YOU

VIOLET.
DON'T LEAVE NOW
JAKE.
NO, VIOLET, NO
I HAVE TO SAY NO TO YOU
DAISY. Jake,
YOU'RE THE ONLY ONE
WHO ALWAYS CARED
VIOLET.
THANK YOU FOR THE LOVE YOU SHARED
JAKE.
WE WERE GOOD FOR EACH OTHER
ALL THE WAY AROUND
YOU WILL FARE WELL

(TERRY and BUDDY enter.)

TERRY.
HAPPY WEDDING DAY!
BUDDY.
WHAT A CROWD OUT THERE!
VIOLET.
BUDDY, GO AWAY
BAD LUCK
IF YOU SEE ME TODAY
BUDDY.
OLD WIVES' TALES DON'T APPLY
VIOLET.
GET OUT, BUDDY
GOOD-BYE
TERRY.
IS SOMETHING WRONG?
DAISY.
JAKE'S LEAVING
VIOLET.
HE'S GOT A JOB IN CHICAGO
TERRY.
JAKE'S NOT GOING ANYWHERE
JAKE.
THIS DOESN'T CONCERN YOU
TERRY.
WHAT CONCERNS THEM
CONCERNS ME

JAKE.
YOU ONLY CARE
HOW BIG HEADLINES WILL BE
TERRY.
I DON'T NEED THIS
GO AHEAD
LEAVE
GOOD RIDDANCE
JAKE.
WHEN I'M GOOD AND READY
TERRY.
YOUR TIMING IS LOUSY
JAKE.
I DON'T PLAY BY YOUR SCRIPT
TERRY.
THEN GO, JAKE
JAKE.
DON'T TELL ME WHAT TO DO
TERRY.
I STILL CALL THE SHOTS HERE
JAKE.
NOT ANYMORE
VIOLET.
STOP IT, YOU TWO
NOT ON MY WEDDING DAY
    JAKE. I'm sorry. Buddy, you be good to Violet. She deserves better.
    BUDDY. Now wait just a minute ...
    JAKE. I'm waiting for you to tell the truth.
    TERRY. Get the hell out of here.

(#27 "Buddy's Confession")

    JAKE. *(To BUDDY.)*
IF YOU HURT HER
I WILL HUNT YOU DOWN

(JAKE exits.)

    TERRY. What was that all about?
    DAISY.
HE LOVES HER
HE TRULY DOES

TERRY. What?!
BUDDY.
HE'S RIGHT, VIOLET
YOU DESERVE BETTER
     TERRY. Buddy!
     BUDDY.
I'VE TRIED
BUT I'M PLAYING A PART
I'VE TRIED
AND IT'S BREAKING MY HEART
     VIOLET.
YOU DON'T LOVE ME?
     BUDDY.
I DO, VIOLET
BUT NOT THE WAY YOU WANT
I'M NOT THAT STRONG OF A MAN
     VIOLET.
BUT YOU'RE THE MAN I LOVE
     BUDDY.
YOU SHOULD BE LOVED
BY SOMEONE LIKE JAKE
SOMEBODY STRONG
WHO'S ABLE TO TAKE
WHATEVER COMES ALONG

SHARING LIFE WITH TWO
IS MORE THAN I CAN DO
IF ONLY I'D KNOWN IT BEFORE
LOVING YOU IS MORE
THAN I BARGAINED FOR
     TERRY. Buddy, get a hold of yourself!
     BUDDY. I have.
     TERRY. Daisy, talk to her. Damn it! This wedding is going to
happen!

(A MAN enters.)

     MAN. Excuse me
     TERRY. No one's allowed back here!
     MAN. Terry Connor?
     TERRY. What?
     BROWNING. Tod Browning from MGM.
     TERRY. Mr. Browning!

DAISY. The movie director?
BROWNING. And you must be the Hilton Sisters. Lovely. Lovely.
BUDDY. And I'm Buddy Foster. I'm the ... groom.
VIOLET. No you're not. No you're not! The wedding is off.
TERRY. Violet!
BROWNING. Did I hear you correctly?
VIOLET. Yes, you did.
BROWNING. What a shame. I came all the way from Hollywood. I intended to offer you roles in my new film.
DAISY. We can still be in your film.
BROWNING. I don't know—without the publicity from the wedding.

(#28 "Marry Me, Terry")

DAISY.
I HAVE A SOLUTION
MARRY ME, TERRY
  TERRY.
WITH THE WHOLE WORLD
EXPECTING A DIFFERENT PAIR?
  DAISY.
THEY'RE EXPECTING THE WEDDING OF A SIAMESE TWIN
THEY WON'T CARE
  BROWNING. Smart girl!
  DAISY.
MARRY ME, TERRY
IT MAKES SO MUCH SENSE
I KNOW YOU WANT ME
JUMP OFF THE FENCE
THE CROWD WANTS A WEDDING
THE BRIDE HAS WITHDRAWN
MARRY ME, TERRY
THE SHOW MUST GO ON
  BROWNING. Marry her, Connor. This story's too big to lose.
  DAISY. No! Do it because you love me.
MARRY ME, TERRY
NO NEED TO PRETEND
I KNOW YOU WANT ME
AS MORE THAN A FRIEND
LAST NIGHT YOU SHOWED
WHAT YOU'RE CAPABLE OF
HAVE YOU FORGOTTEN
THE TUNNEL OF LOVE?

TERRY.
I WAS WEAK
DAISY.
NO—STRONG
TERRY.
I LOST CONTROL
DAISY.
WAS THAT WRONG?
TERRY.
YES IT WAS
DAISY.
BUT WHY?
TERRY.
NOT THE BEHAVIOR
OF A NORMAL GUY
DAISY. Normal?
FEELING LOVE IS NORMAL
HIDING IT IS NOT
WHY CAN'T YOU DISPLAY
THE LOVE YOU KNOW WE'VE GOT
THOUGHT YOU WERE MADE
OF THE STUFF IT WOULD TAKE
MY MISTAKE

MARRY YOU, TERRY?
NOT ON YOUR LIFE
I WOULD BE CRAZY
TO BE YOUR WIFE
WHO IS THE FREAK HERE
THE COWARD, THE LOUT?
MARRY YOU, TERRY?
NO, I WANT YOU OUT!
    BROWNING. Oh for Pete's sake, I'll marry one of 'em!
    DAISY. That won't be necessary.
VIOLET'S MARRYING BUDDY AFTER ALL
    VIOLET. I am not!
    DAISY.
YES YOU ARE
I STEPPED TO THE SIDE
FOR YOUR DREAM
YOU CAN DO THE SAME FOR MINE
    VIOLET. I can't pretend ...

DAISY. Yes, you can!
BUDDY. Do I have anything to say about this?
DAISY. Buddy, you love her. And the most decent thing you can do for all of us, not to mention your own future, is to go through with the ceremony.
BUDDY. Is that what you want, Violet?
VIOLET. Yes.
DAISY. Mr. Browning, you've got your movie stars.
TERRY. You and I can discuss the contract after the ceremony.
DAISY. No you won't. We're through working together.
TERRY. Daisy, please let me do this for you. Let's not confuse emotions with business.
DAISY. Oh, I'm not confused. I don't want to work with you. Mr. Browning, what's the title of our film?
BROWNING. *Freaks.*

(BROWNING exits, then BUDDY and TERRY.)

    VIOLET.
WHAT HAVE WE DONE?
    DAISY.
LEARNED THE TRUTH
    VIOLET.
CLOSED A DOOR
    DAISY.
OPENED MORE
    VIOLET.
I'M SCARED, DAISY
    DAISY.
OF WHAT?
    VIOLET.
BEING ALONE
    DAISY.
BUT YOU'RE NOT
YOU NEVER HAVE BEEN

(#29 "I Will Never Leave You")

    DAISY. (Cont.)
IF WE STOOD ON OUR TIPTOES
WE COULD PEEK OVER THE SILL
AND ONCE IN A WHILE
WE WOULD SEE A GIRL

DAISY. (Cont.)
SLOWLY WALKING UP THE HILL
   VIOLET.
AND WE'D THINK
WHAT A SAD SITUATION
TO BE OUTSIDE ON YOUR OWN
   DAISY.
TO GO THROUGH THE TOWN
WITH NO PLAYMATE
   VIOLET.
TO GO THROUGH LIFE
ALL ALONE
   DAISY and VIOLET.
I WILL NEVER LEAVE YOU
I WILL NEVER GO AWAY
WE WERE MEANT TO SHARE EACH MOMENT
BESIDE YOU IS WHERE I WILL STAY
EVERMORE AND ALWAYS
WE'LL BE ONE THOUGH WE'RE TWO
FOR I WILL NEVER LEAVE YOU
   DAISY.
WHEN THE DAY IS FILLED WITH SHADOWS
WHICH STRETCH INTO THE NIGHT
   VIOLET.
I AM FILLED WITH YOUR SWEET COMFORT
LIKE MORNING FILLS WITH LIGHT
   DAISY and VIOLET.
I WILL NEVER LEAVE YOU
I WILL NEVER GO AWAY
WE WERE MEANT TO SHARE EACH MOMENT
BESIDE YOU IS WHERE I WILL STAY
EVERMORE AND ALWAYS
WE'LL BE ONE THOUGH WE'RE TWO
FOR I WILL NEVER LEAVE YOU

DAISY.	**VIOLET.**
I WILL NEVER LEAVE YOU	
	I WILL NEVER LEAVE YOU
I WILL NEVER GO AWAY	... NEVER GO AWAY

   DAISY and VIOLET.
WE WERE MEANT TO SHARE EACH MOMENT

DAISY.	**VIOLET.**
BESIDE YOU IS WHERE I WILL STAY	
	THAT'S WHERE I WILL STAY

DAISY. (Cont.)   **VIOLET.** (Cont.)
EVERMORE AND ALWAYS
                                  EVERMORE
DAISY and VIOLET.
WE'LL BE ONE THOUGH WE'RE TWO
DAISY.   **VIOLET.**
ONE THOUGH WE'RE TWO
                                  FOR ...
DAISY and VIOLET.
I WILL NEVER
I WILL NEVER
I WILL NEVER LEAVE YOU

*(DAISY and VIOLET pivot and walk Upstage as the ROUSTABOUTS
reconfigure the set to mirror the beginning of the show. After a
moment to compose themselves, DAISY and VIOLET pivot again
and cross Downstage as in a wedding procession.)*

(#29 "Wedding Processional")

Scene 11 - THE STADIUM

(#30 "Daisy, Can You Hear What I'm Thinking?")

VIOLET.
DAISY, CAN YOU HEAR WHAT I'M THINKING?
DAISY.
YES, CLEARLY AS THOUGH YOU SPOKE
VIOLET.
GIVE ME STRENGTH, I FEEL MY SPIRITS SINKING
DAISY.
TRY TO LAUGH
THIS IS THE BIGGEST JOKE
WE HAVE SEEN THE WORLD
VIOLET.
AND IT'S SEEN US
DAISY.
WE HAVE CAUSED A SCENE

VIOLET.
WE HAVE MADE A FUSS
ARE WE EVER TO LEARN
WHY WE'VE LIVED AS TWO
   DAISY.
PROBABLY NOT
BUT I'M THANKFUL
   BOTH.
IT'S BEEN WITH YOU
   DAISY.
COME LOOK AT THE FREAKS
   VIOLET.
BEFORE THEY'RE ANTIQUES
   DAISY and VIOLET.
COME AND GIVE THEM A STRONG OVATION
AN ACCLAMATION
BUT NO CRITIQUES
   DAISY.
SEE WHAT HOLLYWOOD SEEKS
   DAISY and VIOLET.
COME LOOK AT THE FREAKS

(The COMPANY enters. The ROUSTABOUTS complete reconfiguring the set as at the beginning of the show.)

Scene 12 - AS IN PROLOGUE

THE BOSS. *(Offstage. Over an echoing microphone.)* Good people, we are gathered here today to join two souls as one. If there be anyone present who knows of a reason these two should not be joined together let him speak now or forever hold his peace.

DAISY, VIOLET and COMPANY.
AH, AH, AH
AH, AH, AH, AH
AH, AH, AH, AH

(The COMPANY sits as at the top of the show.)

THE BOSS.
COME LOOK AT THE FREAKS   **COMPANY.**
                                      SEE THE BRIDE

COMPANY.
CURIOSITY SATISFIED
COME AND GIVE THEM
A STRONG OVATION
AN ACCLAMATION
BUT NO CRITIQUES

(DAISY and VIOLET split apart and sit.)

COMPANY. (Cont.)
SEE LOVE GLORIFIED
   SEE LOVE GLORIFIED
SEE LOVE GLORIFIED
   SEE LOVE GLORIFIED
COME HEAR HOW LOVE SPEAKS
COME LOOK AT THE FREAKS!

(The COMPANY sits as at the beginning of the show. Blackout.)

END OF PLAY

PROP LIST

Scene I-1A
   1 Big Lollipop- 8" diameter (Dolly Dimples)
   1 Riding Crop
   1 Starter Pistol (The Boss)
   4 Roustabout Dowels - Plus Spares (Roustabouts)
Scene I- 1B
   1 Act One Circus Podium (Daisy and Violet)
   1 Carnie Shadow Cloth - sheet w/two Poles and Velcro
   (Roustabouts -ripped down by The Boss)
Scene I-2
   Cash Bills (Terry)
Scene I-3
   3 Benches (Attractions, 1 for Daisy & Violet)
   2 Birthday Cakes w/10 Candles Each (Dolly Dimples and
   Fortune Teller)
   1 Crown (Jake)
   1 Cigar (Dolly Dimples)
Scene I-5
   2 Wildflower Bouquets (Terry and Buddy)
Scene I-7
   10 Reporter Note Pads & Pencils
   5 Cameras w/Flash Units (Reporters)
Scene I-8
   Camera w/Flash Unit (Photographer)
Scene I-10
   6 Oars
   2 Egyptian Fans
Scene I-11
   5 Cameras w/Flash Units (Reporters)
Scene II-1
   1 Act II Follies "Circus" Podium (Daisy and Violet)
Scene II-5
   4 30's Microphones w/Stands [Non Functional] (Daisy, Violet,
   Buddy, Vale Sisters)
   2 Stools (Daisy and Violet)

COSTUME LIST

DAISY AND VIOLET HILTON

I-1 (Prologue)
  30s style dress; Styled wig

I-1b (Inside the tent)
  Nude leotard and hose; Stringy wig

I-3 (Behind the Tent)
  Chemise; Lace-up boots

I-5 (Dressing area)
  Cotton robe; Same wig as I-1

I-6 (In the tent)
  Home-made performance costume

I-8 (Photo shoot)
  Dressy afternoon dress

I-10 (Vaudeville)
  Egyptian dress, headress, wig

I-11 (Backstage)
  Dressy dress

II-1 (The Follies)
  Bird-like dress; Feathered head-dress

II-3 (New Year's Eve)
  Evening gown; Stole or maribu; Gloves

II-4 ("Private Conversation")
  Black slip

II-5 ("One Plus One Equals Three")
  Skirt, jacket, vest and hat; Stole or shrug; Gloves

II-7 ("Tunnel of Love")
  Skirt and sweater ensemble

II-10 (The wedding)
  Cream or white dress

TERRY TURNER

I-1a (Outside the tent)
  Wool pants; Sports jacket; Shirt w/tie

I-4 (In the tent)
  Pants, vest and jacket; Shirt and tie

I-7 (Press conference)
  Pants (repeat I-4); Jacket

II-2 (Backstage)
    White tie, tails, vest
II-5 (Radio station)
    Suit and vest; Shirt and tie
II-7 (The Texas Centennial)
    Suit and vest
II-10 (Stadium dressing area)
    Suit and vest; Shirt and tie

BUDDY FOSTER
    I-1a (Outside the tent)
        Pants; T-shirt; Jacket; Boots
    I-4 (In the tent)
        Same as I-1a but with shirt and no jacket
    I-8 (Photo shoot)
        Pants; Shirt; Jacket
    II-2 (Backstage)
        White tie and tails w/vest
    II-5 (On stage)
        Pants and jacket; Vest; Straw boater; Spectator shoes
    II-7 (The Texas Centennial)
        Pants; Shirt
    II-10 (Stadium dressing area)
        Suit and vest; Shirt and tie

JAKE
    I-1 (Prologue)
        Pants; Shirt; Jacket; Cap
    I-1b (Inside the tent)
        Loincloth
        Cuffs w/shackles
    I-3 (Behind the bleachers)
        Overalls; Tank t-shirt
    I-4 (In the tent)
        Overalls (repeat I-3); T-shirt; Vest
    I-8 (Photo shoot)
        Turtleneck; Jacket; Pants from I-1
    II-2 (Backstage)
        White tie and tails; Vest
    II-5 (Onstage)
        Pants and vest; Jacket; Shirt

II-10 (Stadium dressing area)
    Repeat I-1

THE BOSS
I-1 (Prologue)
    Shirt; Pants and jacket; Vest
I-1b (Inside the tent)
    Coat; Vest; Tophat
I-6 (Inside the tent)
    Repeat I-1
II-9 (Outside the Cotton Bowl)
    Repeat I-1b
    Red oversized velvet tophat

FORTUNE TELLER
I-1 (Prologue)
    30s style dress
    Kimono
I-1b (Inside the tent)
    Fortune Teller Dress
    Earrings, necklaces, hair ornaments
I-2 (Behind the tent)
    Slip; Robe
II-1 (Follies)
    Bird costume
II-3 (New Year's Eve)
    Elegan dress and jewelry

DOLLY DIMPLES
I-1 (Prologue)
    Suit; Cape
I-12b (Inside the tent)
    Corset; Girdle
    Peignoir and bonnet
I-2 (Behind the tent)
    Robe
II-1 (Follies)
    Bird costume
II-3 (New Year's Eve)
    Elegant dress and jewelry

6ᵀᴴ EXHIBIT
I-1 (Prologue)
Blouse; Skirt; Coat
I-1b (Inside the tent)
Costume suggesting religious martyr
II-1 (The Follies)
Bird costume
II-3 (New Year's Eve)
Elegant dress

SNAKE LADY
I-1 (Prologue)
Dress and jacket
I-1b (Inside the tent)
Sideshow costume
I-3 (Behind the bleachers)
Pajama pants
Kimono
II-1 (The Follies - Flamingo)
Bird costume
II-3 (New Year's Eve)
Elegant evening attire w/Asian accents

HAREM GIRL 1
I-1 (Prologue)
Skirt and sweater
I-1 (In the tent)
Harem costume
I-3 (Behind the bleachers)
Robe
II-1 (The Follies - Flamingo)
Bird costume
II-3 (New Year's Eve)
Elegant dress

HAREM GIRL 2
I-1 (Prologue)
Skirt and jacket

I-3 (Inside the tent)
    Harem costume
I-3 (Behind the bleachers)
    Robe
II-1 (The Follies - Flamingo)
    Bird costume
II-3 (New Year's Eve)
    Elegant dress

GEEK
    I-1 (Prologue)
        Pants and vest
        Shirt; Duster; Gloves
    I-1b (In the tent)
        Pants
        Bloodied shirt, vest and duster
    1-7 (Press conference)
        Suit; Dickie with tie
        Suspenders and hat
    I-10 (Vaudeville)
        Pharoah costume
    II-1 (The Follies)
        Bird costume
    Ii-3 (New Year's Eve)
        White tie and tails; Vest

BEARDED LADY
    I-1 (Prologue)
        Pants w/suspenders
        Frilly shirt; Vest
    I-1b (Inside the tent)
        Dress w/hoop
        Victorian ringlet wig with hair ornaments
    I-3 (Behind the bleachers)
        Robe (feminine)
    I-7 (Press conference)
        Suit and vest; Shirt; Tie; Hat
    II-1 (The Follies)
        Bird costume
    II-3 (New Year's Eve)
        White tie and tails; Overcoat

REPTILE MAN
    I-1 (Prologue)
        Pants; Sweater
    I-1b (Inside the tent)
        Reptile man costume
    I-7 (Press conference)
        Suit; Dickie w/tie; Hat
    I-10 (Vaudeville)
        Pharoah costume
    II-1 (The Follies)
        Bird costume
    II-3 (New Year's Eve)
        Evening suit

FAKIR
    I-1 (Prologue)
        Pants; Suspenders; Nehru shirt
    I-1b (Inside the tent)
        Fakir costume w/turban
    1-3 (Behind the bleachers)
        Indian robe
    1-7 (Press Conference)
        Suit; Dickie w/tie; Hat
    1-10 (Vaudeville)
        Pharoah costume
    1-11 (The Follies)
        Bird costume
    1-13 (New Years's Eve)
        Elegant suit with accents suggesting India

SHEIK
    I-1 (Prologue)
        Pants; Turtleneck; Suspenders and belt
    I-1b (Inside the tent)
        Sheik costume
    I-3 (Behind the bleachers)
        Pants (distressed)
        Tank top
    I-7 (Press conference)
        Suit; Dickie w/tie; Hat

I-11 (Vaudeville)
    Pharoah costume
II-1 (The Follies)
    Bird costume
II-3 (New Year's Eve)
    White tie and tails; Vest
II-10 (Tod Browning)
    Pinstripe suit and vest; Homburg

ROUSTABOUTS
(Basically the same except for slight variations in I-1 and I-7)
    I-1 (Prologue)
        Shirt; Pants
    I-1b (Inside the tent)
        Roustabout gear
    I-7 (Press conference)
        Dickie w/tie; Suit; Hat
    I-10 (Vaudeville - Archeologist)
        Safari costume w/pith helmet
        (Vaudeville - Pharoah)
        Pharoah costume
    II-1 (The Follies)
        Bird costume
    II-3 (New Year's Eve)
        Tuxedo; Wing collar shirt; Bowtie